The Nordic PhD

This book is part of the Peter Lang Education list.
Every volume is peer reviewed and meets
the highest quality standards for content and production.

PETER LANG
New York • Bern • Frankfurt • Berlin
Brussels • Vienna • Oxford • Warsaw

The Nordic PhD

Surviving and Succeeding

Christopher McMaster, Caterina Murphy,
Jakob Rosenkrantz de Lasson,
Editors

PETER LANG
New York • Bern • Frankfurt • Berlin
Brussels • Vienna • Oxford • Warsaw

Library of Congress Cataloging-in-Publication Data

Names: McMaster, Christopher (Christopher Todd), editor. |
Murphy, Caterina, editor. | de Lasson, Jakob Rosenkrantz, editor.
Title: The Nordic PhD: surviving and succeeding / edited by
Christopher McMaster, Caterina Murphy, and Jakob Rosenkrantz de Lasson.
Description: New York: Peter Lang, 2018.
Includes bibliographical references.
Identifiers: LCCN 2017039291 | ISBN 978-1-4331-4823-1 (hardback) |
ISBN 978-1-4331-5004-3 (pbk.: alk. paper) | ISBN 978-1-4331-5018-0 (ebook pdf) |
ISBN 978-1-4331-5019-7 (epub) | ISBN 978-1-4331-5020-3 (mobi)
Subjects: LCSH: Universities and colleges—Scandinavia—Graduate work. |
Doctor of philosophy degree—Scandinavia. | Doctoral students—Scandinavia. |
Academic thesis—Scandinavia.
Classification: LCC LB2371.6.S33 N67 | DDC 378.20948—dc23
LC record available at https://lccn.loc.gov/2017039291
DOI 10.3726/b11985

Bibliographic information published by **Die Deutsche Nationalbibliothek.**
Die Deutsche Nationalbibliothek lists this publication in the "Deutsche
Nationalbibliografie"; detailed bibliographic data are available
on the Internet at http://dnb.d-nb.de/.

29 Broadway, 18th floor, New York, NY 10006
www.peterlang.com

To the many doctoral students and graduates who contributed to this book in order to help future doctoral students survive and succeed in PhD programs in the Nordic countries.

Table of Contents

Foreword

Enjoy the Journey

LENE TANGGAARD AND CHARLOTTE WEGENER

This book covers a range of questions and issues related to taking on, surviving and finishing a PhD. Taking a specifically Nordic view of doctoral studies, it addresses a range of questions students in the Nordic countries have asked themselves and others on the journey towards a finished thesis. What is specifically *Nordic* about a Nordic PhD? What does it mean to survive and succeed, and how can one stay the course and make it as a doctoral researcher in a Nordic country? The collection of texts in this book offers a variety of answers and leaves the reader with a nuanced image of the Nordic collaborative mentality and research practice. It embraces an abundance of perspectives on the doctoral journey, some of which have a particularly 'Nordic' take, while others are of a more general character. They will help you understand and navigate the often-complex process of getting started, working on and finishing a PhD. In a sense, the authors write with the intention of making the process easier and more transparent for other students by sharing their own stories, their hopes, dreams, sorrows and difficulties as they were encountered and managed as part of their own PhD endeavours.

You may think that a book on the Nordic PhD addresses a narrow audience up North. This is far from the case. The book is aimed at those around the world who are considering doctoral studies and those who have already settled in a Nordic country to study for a doctorate. Why go? Why stay? Nordic research life holds rewards and perils. From these chapters, you will learn that we have rather non-hierarchical and informal working cultures. You will learn that autonomy is honoured, which means that you are rather free but also risk being lonely. Education is free but everything else is expensive. Winter is hard but there are cosy lunch and coffee breaks—and you should never regard it as a waste of time to take part!

There is a lot of advice to be found in this book, and advice is always tricky. We may not learn from others just because they tell us what to do. We need to walk the paths ourselves, navigate by our own beacons, stumble, and learn from it all. Therefore, this book is not just *about* the Nordic PhD. It is a genuine product of the non-hierarchical and informal Nordic mentality. The authors are speaking straight from their own doctoral experience; their voices resonate with us because they are right beside us, their readers. The contributors share their various perspectives and experiences, not as teachers, but as peers. This is close-up and personal advice from people who are travelling the Nordic landscape of doctoral research themselves—as natives or as newcomers.

As Nordic natives, we have learned about our own particularly Nordic take on research life only by travelling abroad. We started working together as supervisor and doctoral researcher and soon built a straightforward, fruitful and fun partnership around our shared interest in creativity, innovation and learning. Not least, we found that co-writing was productive, and we presented a paper about student-supervisor co-writing at an American conference (later published as Wegener & Tanggaard, 2013). This paper told the story of the apprenticeship-like relationship evolving around our collaboration as supervisor and student, and in particular how we collaborated on an almost equal footing when writing papers. We wrote about co-writing in a general sense, but, after presenting the paper to an American audience, we realized that there was something Nordic about our relationship. The American students and professors attending our presentation asked us to write more about this, as they saw a huge need for less hierarchical and more equal supervision as part of the doctoral journey. Inspired, we flew back to Denmark and began to work on a new book: "*A Survival Kit for Doctoral Students and their Supervisors*" (Tanggaard & Wegener, 2016). We are therefore excited to see this Nordic take on the doctoral process get even more attention with this great book on the Nordic PhD.

Generally, there is a need to understand the landscape around doctoral studies, including the geographical and cultural aspects. What we take for granted in our home countries may appear strange to foreigners. As one of our colleagues born in Eastern Europe once said to us, 'I really do not understand the kind of freedom you have here. What am I supposed to do?' While we often enjoy a lot of freedom in our workplaces, it comes with obligations often only spoken of indirectly. This kind of cultural code is good to know if one is to navigate new territory successfully. This is true when the territory is a new country, but equally true when entering a new organization and building a new identity as a doctoral researcher.

That said, there is no such thing as *a* Nordic take on the doctoral process. Although we are similar in many ways, we also like to tease our Nordic neighbours about their food preferences, comment on their strange sense of humour, and compete fiercely with each other in contests of all kinds. The Nordic countries differ from one another in many ways, just as each university and each research group is different. Moreover, it is never solely a question of fitting in: culture is not static, and we as newcomers may bring about change, too. It is good to think about the kind of change one would like to represent.

As it is everywhere in the world, doctoral research in a Nordic country is demanding, at times a struggle, but also rewarding and fun. Fun and rewards are found when pursuing creativity, thinking wildly and getting involved in supportive teams and relationships. This book is a great companion for the Nordic PhD endeavour. With this in your luggage, you are encouraged not only to survive and succeed, but to actually enjoy the journey.

References

Tanggaard, L., & Wegener, C. (2016). *A survival kit for doctoral students and their supervisors. Travelling the landscape of research.* Thousand Oaks, CA: SAGE.

Wegener, C., & Tanggaard, L. (2013). Supervisor and student co-writing: An apprenticeship perspective. *Forum Qualitative Sozialforschung / Forum: Qualitative Social Research, 14*(3). Retrieved from http://www.qualitative-research.net/index.php/fqs/article/view/2030

Preface and Acknowledgments

The Nordic PhD: Surviving and Succeeding is the sixth edition in the global *Survive and Succeed* series, following editions from New Zealand, Australia, South Africa, the UK and the USA (2014, 2016, 2017). The book was originally envisioned as a Scandinavian edition in the series, but this was changed to a Nordic edition, as contributors come from both Scandinavia (Denmark, Norway and Sweden) and other northern countries (Finland and Iceland). Throughout the book the terms Nordic and Scandinavia are used.

In August 2014, a call for abstracts for the Australian edition was posted by the Thesis Whisperer, an Australian blog for postgraduate students, and after reading this, Jakob, who at that point was doing a PhD in Denmark, contacted Chris and Caterina to learn more. Soon, the idea of a Nordic edition was conceived, and book development began.

Each contributor is a current PhD student or recent graduate. When invited to submit an abstract, they were asked: 'What do you wish you had known when you started your own PhD project? What advice would you give yourself, if able to go back in time to when you started?'

Each chapter is practice focussed rather than theory focussed, and contains down-to-earth and ready-to-use advice on many aspects of PhD student life. While each chapter is written by a person with experience from a specific field—for example, the natural or technical sciences or the humanities—we have strived to make the advice relevant and applicable regardless of your own field of study, and we believe that all current and prospective PhD students can benefit from the advice offered by each contributor. While there are differences between the Nordic countries and between their PhD systems, specific facts about individual countries have, to the best of our ability, been pointed out. There are important aspects of each system and culture that create a platform for shared experience.

The Nordic PhD consists of 18 chapters which are divided into five parts. The first part focuses on practical matters of the PhD, with chapters on note taking, technological tools and thesis writing. Part 2 is concerned with new opportunities, such as returning to academia after a break, or starting a PhD in a new field. The third part covers wellbeing and support, such as staying well during your studies, and pursuing a PhD in a Nordic country with a physical or mental disability. Relationships are the topic of Part 4, where, among others, the nature of supervisor relations is covered. Part 5 describes and delivers advice to international students coming to a Nordic country to engage in PhD study. *The Nordic PhD: Surviving and Succeeding* is a platform, where prospective and current students can come together and benefit from the advice within its pages.

Editing a book is often, as in this case, a spare time activity for us as editors. Therefore, there are some acknowledgments that must be expressed.

Firstly, we wish to thank all the contributing authors, without whom this book would not have eventuated. It has been a pleasure for us as editors to work with you on this project.

A special thank you to Natacha (Jakob's wife) for her patience, understanding and support when spending another evening or weekend on the book.

A special thank you also to Anthony (Caterina's husband) and Wendy (Chris' wife) for their ongoing support and patience throughout the development of the *Survive and Succeed* series. It has been a long road travelled, and we are pleased that the *Survive and Succeed* series has come to the Nordic region of Earth.

NB: While the editors appreciate and accept the significant contribution of each chapter to the book as a whole, they do not necessarily endorse all viewpoints expressed within them.

References

Frick, L., Motshoane, P., McMaster, C., & Murphy, C. (Eds.). (2016). *Postgraduate study in South Africa: Surviving and succeeding*. Cape Town: SunMedia.

McMaster, C., & Murphy, C. (Eds.). (2014). *Postgraduate study in Aotearoa New Zealand: Surviving and succeeding*. Wellington: NZCER Press.

McMaster, C., & Murphy, C. (Eds.). (2016). *Graduate study in the USA: Surviving and succeeding*. New York, NY: Peter Lang Publishing.

McMaster, C., Murphy, C., Cronshaw, S., & Codiroli-McMaster, N. (Eds.). (2017). *Postgraduate study in the UK: Surviving and succeeding*. London: Libris Press.

McMaster, C., Murphy, C., Mewburn, I., & Whitburn, B. (Eds.). (2017). *Postgraduate study in Australia: Surviving and succeeding*. New York, NY: Peter Lang Publishing.

PART ONE

Practical Matters

CHAPTER ONE

Technological Tools for 21st Century PhDs

SIMON KROGH

Introduction

Starting work on a PhD thesis can be a daunting task. You may be excited about having come this far; your funding might be sorted, and you might even have your topic and approach defined. You are all set to go, but then what? Do you just start reading whatever you come across? Perhaps your supervisor has given you a couple of articles to read, or perhaps you turn to some of your old books to get some familiar, firm ground to start from? This chapter will discuss how you can get started by taking a closer look at the indispensable technological academic tools for note taking (e.g. MS OneNote, Evernote), reference management (e.g. Mendeley, Refworks), citations (Databases) and analytics (Nvivo, Atlas Ti, SPSS).

It should not be taken for granted that your new colleagues or your supervisor at the University use or even know these tools. They have their own academic preferences and habits and if they got their academic degrees several years ago they may have stuck with the methods and tools they used back then, rather than embracing what is available now. An impressive collection of books and many years of experience is by no means a guarantee of good working methods. This chapter suggests that it is important to learn new and smarter ways of academic study. Like other professions, academics also need a toolbox containing indispensable research tools. I will highlight the four types of software tools that I have experienced and believe make a real difference in the effort to complete a PhD thesis.

A proper command of essential tools will allow the academic thinker to work much smarter. The time you spend in the early days in getting yourself and your work organized will reward you many fold near the end when you really need the time and you are pressured to complete your thesis.

The library of your university will most likely have lists of essential academic tools. They may even offer courses. But if you are like most people, you will 'skip the manual', which in academic terms translates into not bothering to learn the appropriate tools and move straight to books and start reading. Keep in mind that you can read until your funds run dry and not accomplish anything, if the reading does not translate into writing. This is where the tools come into play.

Note Taking: Don't Trust Your Memory

One of the inevitable aspects of a PhD journey is the mind-numbing amount of information you are expected to absorb, like the number of academic articles, books and scientific reports, not to mention media stories and other 'soft' sources that you may come across. One of the first things you need to do is stop believing that you can actually remember everything—even when you read something that you find extraordinarily interesting and are sure that you will remember once you have 'just finished this other bit'. We have all experienced that despite the best intentions to get back to it again … we don't, because we get caught up in the next interesting detail. There is always more to read, and the sooner you realize that you cannot trust your memory the better.

You need a technological tool that will help you remember stuff and luckily help is at hand as there is a variety of software products to choose from in regards to note taking. Whether you choose Evernote, Microsoft OneNote, Apple Notes (or one of the many options you can choose) they are essentially all just advanced notepads that will allow you to take notes. You can copy and paste from research papers. Capture screenshots and anything else you need to keep. The really clever part of it is that you have everything in one place and you can make intelligent searches across a variety of materials. You can essentially return to your own thoughts, even if you had forgotten about them. The important thing is to keep taking notes from the start and throughout your project. Chapter 2 will look at note taking software in more detail.

Regardless of which note-taking-tool you choose the beginning is quite easy. Things are interesting and the start-up energy is still there. You read something, make a few notes under an illustrative heading. It is when you get to your entry number 10 and 20 that you need to stick with it. Stay systematic and trust the value of your own thinking. The notes you are making are valuable. Think of it as the crops you start harvesting and keep in your storage. At first you are excited and can see the progress. But as the storage gradually fills and you are not really using any of it, doubts will start to creep in—or perhaps even laziness. In the myriads of research papers on your desk or on your computer it can be hard to tell what is important and what is not. You may come to a point where you think that you have already gathered enough thoughts and reflections based on readings, fieldtrips or late night flashes of inspiration. Don't stop taking notes. Keep collecting thoughts, because you will need them as your work progresses and moves into a more structured analysis and writing.

Imagine that you are two years into your PhD study. The deadline is still just a thought or it could be that it starts lurking in the horizon. There you are—Wednesday morning at the coffee machine talking to a colleague and all of a sudden you recall something about a particular topic you are working on and you know you read an article about it and had some really good reflections. If you have stuck with your thinking tools from the start and taken good notes this is where it starts to pay off. This is where it becomes clear that yellow post-it notes on the side of the monitor have limitations and that e-mails written to yourself tend to disappear in a sea of other e-mails. The structured notes, taken in a proper note-taking-tool, which can be searched and include screen shots and links to media files, suddenly become a valuable source of insight and reflection. Keep in mind that good thinking and good writing are intrinsically linked (Huff, 1999). They are not separate processes. Developing ideas happens in an intricate interaction between thinking and seeing what you have just written. Ask yourself, 'How can I know what I think until I see what I write?' (Huff, 1999; Weick, 1995).

Reference Manager: Yes, You Need It!

A reference manager is a simple way to keep track of your references and make sure that you adhere to the standards of academia in terms of referencing. You can think of the reference manager as you own personal librarian. The reference manager will help you make sure that you follow the APA-standard if required, and at the press of a button you can change to Harvard-style if this is needed. The reference manager helps to make sure that your references are up to date, and that you will not miss that important reference in a last minute attempt to do things manually. It is only when things start to get a bit complex, and the number of references start to rise, that you really start to appreciate the significance of the reference manager.

A typical example of how a reference manager can be used starts with you reading something interesting. Then, there is something that needs to be investigated further. Once you have found the book or article and have identified it as relevant, type it into your reference manager. Download the text and include it in your reference manager and make your annotations directly in the document in the reference manager. Working this way will save you time, and if you have your note-taking-program running simultaneously the process of reading, thinking, writing and managing becomes integrated and more efficient.

One of the concerns often raised in relation to reference managers is whether you can actually trust them. What if the codes get all screwed up and my document gets corrupted? Will I lose everything? There are so many aspects of modern life we take for granted and for the academic, the reference manager ought to be one of them. You don't bring a generator to work out of fear of a power cut.

Citation Databases: Who Said That?

Citation databases will essentially help you figure out who is quoting who in academia. If you have read a book or an article and wonder who else referred to it you will need to use citation databases. In other words, they are online tools and resources that will make it easier to achieve consistency and thoroughness in your writing. Granted, sometimes when things are easy it almost feels like cheating and writing a PhD should not be easy. It is perhaps the most important thing you will ever write, and at times you may feel like just getting up and leaving. Reading one article after the other can be a cumbersome task. The amount of information and the number of articles and books available is virtually limitless, and still you have to work your way through it. This cannot be avoided at this level of academic pursuit.

I like to think of it as digging deeper and deeper into the ground. You can dig a hole with your hands, but if you have shovel (a tool) it is just much more efficient. Think of citation databases as the tools that allow you to dig into the endless amounts articles and books that are required to write a proper PhD-dissertation. You have to find a way through what exists in your field of research. The efficient way to do this is to look at what everybody else is referring to. If everybody else is referring to a few articles, they are probably important. If a journal in your field is higher ranked than all the others, then it is probably because it contains texts that are more significant than the others. If an author has many citations and is always referenced by everybody else, then they are probably a good place to start. By using the citation databases of your specific field, you will be able to draw lines from the classics to the most recent research in your field. All this sifting back and forth from classics to cutting edge is where you are going to need the citation databases. They will allow you to get an overview of what is out there.

In a sense, the citation database will ensure that you get through all the things you must. By relying on citation databases for identifying the bulk of the important stuff, you will have freed-up time to focus on more specialized articles, those that nobody else had spotted as important and will eventually set your work apart.

Analytical Tools: Hmmm, I See!

A core element of any PhD thesis is analysis, which can be conducted in numerous ways. Moving into the 21st century, we have analytical tools available that will allow us to gain insights into data that no manual or analogue method could ever do.

A typical approach to start working on a PhD is by reading up on theories. You might do your literature review and then start gathering data, or you might do it simultaneously. Once you have the theoretical foundation in place and once you have pulled together some of your data you move on to the more structured analysis. This is the tough part of the PhD work, but also the most rewarding.

If you gather quantitative data, you will need software like IBM SPSS to help you crunch the numbers (links and descriptions are offered at the end of Chapter 2). In a qualitative study, where data typically consists of unstructured data, analytical tools can also be very helpful and there are plenty available on the market. Atlas Ti, MaxQDA and Nvivo … just to mention a few. These Qualitative Data Analysis (QDA) tools will allow you to upload a variety of qualitative data, including interview transcripts, newspaper articles, academic journals and video and audio clips. The tools make it possible to structure, code, query data and identify patterns in the data that are hidden under the surface of a large data set. Cleverly designed queries might reveal patterns across many interviews that are not visible in individual interviews. But don't be mistaken—you still have to do the analysis. QDA tools do not relieve you from doing the analysis, but if you are able to ask clever question to your data the QDA-tool will be able to return insightful answers. Some QDA tools are quite expensive, and each have their strengths and weaknesses so your best bet is to get in touch with your library and check which solution is supported (and paid for) by your institution in the first instance.

Some colleagues will tell you stories about how they print out transcriptions of interviews and lay them out on the floor before sorting the data. Work smarter in a day and age where software applications can make the process of analysis so much easier. Modern computers equipped with the right analytical software will allow you to gain insights into data that manual methods could never do.

Conclusion

Regardless of what direction your PhD study takes you, all academics have two things in common. We develop new knowledge by remembering things and thinking about stuff. This is the essence of becoming an academic scholar. In the finest of moments, your PhD may resemble art and feel like inspiration from above. More often, however, it is just hard work and an effort to stay motivated and focused. It is when you are in the 'hard-work-zone' of your PhD study, that you will truly appreciate the strength of good technological tools. If you have the tools mastered in the early parts of your PhD journey you will have freed up valuable thinking time for the later parts. Don't trust your memory—put your faith in tools that will help you think and remember.

References

Huff, A. S. (1999). *Writing for scholary publications*. Thousand Oaks, CA: Sage Publications.
Weick, K. E. (1995). *Sensemaking in organizations*. Thousand Oaks, CA: Sage Publications.

CHAPTER TWO

Paper Is Power

The Art of Making Notes

JULIAN GEIGER

Introduction

Making notes is an everyday activity at universities. Even though writing things down might seem like a trivial task, the quality and usability of notes is extremely important. Not surprisingly, many students (including myself) have frequent thoughts like, 'Oh, why did I not make a note of this?' The value of putting pieces of information properly down and marking details systematically on a sheet of paper cannot be ignored by the doctoral student.

Paper is power. I first heard this magical phrase in a course about project work. At the time, it struck me as an abstract concept with no practical meaning. But a few months of study taught me otherwise. One of my favorite examples illustrating the impact of a few written lines comes from the TV-series *The Big Bang Theory*. Sheldon goes through journals he wrote as a child and explains to his roommate:

> In 1964, Dr. Peter Higgs, accomplished self-promoter and physicist, wrote a paper postulating the existence of a subatomic particle called the Higgs boson. Now, initially the paper was rejected, but recently he was proven right, and now he's on the fast track to win a Nobel prize. ... The point is: Higgs is being celebrated for work he did 50 years ago, so that got me thinking, perhaps I've already hit upon the idea that will win me my Nobel Prize. (Cendrowski, Lore, & Prady, 2012)

Notes are a valuable tool for every academic, from student to professor, regardless of whether they aim for a Nobel Prize or just passing the next exam. You just need to know when and how to take them. This chapter outlines how to master the art of taking notes. It focuses on note taking when reading literature, for documenting and analyzing experiments, during supervision and when participating in conferences. By the end of the chapter you will know how to start harvesting the potential of notes for your academic life.

Reading: On the Lookout for Know-How

Setting sails in a new sea of study—whether in science, humanities, economics or any other field—will include the need to familiarize yourself with current and past literature. A fair share of time will be spent on reading, no matter what discipline you are in. During the years as a doctoral student, I went through *a lot* of texts, most of them in the form of electronic documents, and as a consequence the number of PDF files on my computer increased tremendously. To conquer this armada of files in a long-term accessible and sustainable way, I started to use a reference manager to keep track of references and organize them in a systematic way. For the specific choice of reference manager, I came to like Mendeley, but alternatives exist such as Zotero, EndNote, BibDesk, JabRef, and Papers. A strong argument for my choice of Mendeley was the possibility to synchronize my complete references in one single BibTex format file; this was the most convenient format for inclusion in my thesis work which was written in the typesetting language LaTeX. It does not matter which reference manager you use as long as it works for you and allows you to anchor your reference library in a systematical way. Just find and proceed with the tool best suited for your specific way of working and needs. To make your choice, look at reviews of different tools to make an informed choice. Your choice may also be dictated by the software used at your institution, and descriptions and links to many are offered at the end of this chapter.

Certain reference managers, including Mendeley, have automatic detection and management of bibliographic data (such as author, journal, year) from imported PDFs, which is convenient as it makes handling of new references smoother. References can then be sorted in different folders, each corresponding to different topics or projects, and where references can be put into several project folders. Alternatively, a web-importer tool can be used to save web-side based references into a personal library while browsing. My most used feature in Mendeley was adding annotations to articles in a separate window while reading them; all my notes on literature have been taken in that way.

Annotations can be made in a multitude of ways; simply find the technique that works for you. I typically use bullet points and summarize which contents are new to me, how the main findings relate to my project, and which methods are used to obtain the results. I start my notes with the name of the article and also sometimes add important terms. When planning to write a literature review, for a paper or for your thesis, such terms and key words in a separate list of 'typical expressions' is useful in building systematic search queries.

A reference manager's search function can also be useful. If you, like me, use certain words or an interesting thought from articles rather than the particular reference, adding such key terms as annotations is an advantage. Via the search function, a particular article is easily found from the library.

When reading literature, pay attention to the vocabulary, phrases and language style of publications, especially if you are a non-native English speaker, as this can alleviate the limits of active vocabulary during writing. Compile a list of typical expressions from the literature to conclude, summarize, reason, etc. If your work includes visualization of data, find inspiration in figures and tables in references during reading. When you stumble upon an elegant or intelligent presentation in a reference, make a note and refer back to it when making your own figures or tables. Use your annotations and comments actively and browse through them on a regular basis—an approach that is excellently described in the article, *On Intellectual Craftsmanship* (Mills, 1980). By carefully taking notes, you shape a personal resource pool that goes beyond pure academic information.

Experiments: Journey Beyond the Horizon of Current Knowledge

A core principle in many disciplines is to generate a hypothesis from observations and afterwards test it. Testing can be done in many ways, including lab experiments, surveys, interviews, or web-searches. Notes are of great value and can contribute to the planning, execution and documentation processes. While my own study was grounded in quantitative methodology, the note taking habits discussed below can also apply to qualitative data gathering and analysis.

Start your notes on the very first day in a new research project or group. Thorough notes taken during or at the end of the day are a good start: Who did you talk to? Which position did the person have? Where can you find equipment and different facilities? Where is the next printer? Who do you talk to about office supplies? Write it all down. Once you have started your research project, keep a track record of your daily work. In the sciences, it is common to keep a hard copy lab journal with documentation of all performed experiments (Thomson, 2007). But also keep notes on experiments in electronic folders. Give each experiment its own folder that contains all relevant information in subfolders: experimental setup, primary results, data analysis and everything else. The hard copy journal can be expanded into a general log-book of daily labors summarizing important details. Track how much time you spend on different activities. Document your search queries, key words, and databases used for information retrieving. Write down any addresses of useful resources and web pages that you discover. Based on log entries, identify repeated tasks. For my own work, I developed an easy-to-follow manual (my 'Standard Operating Procedure') and template sheets for such routines. Designing file templates is a simple one-time chore in standard office programs like Excel or Word. Creating stand-alone notes and self-explanatory instructions for colleagues and students helps to save a lot of time.

Data Analysis: Deciphering the Map

Expeditions on unknown regions of research go hand in hand with collecting data. New data must be analyzed and merged with previous facts to reach a more complete map. Data can be collected in many ways: as output from measuring instruments, computer simulations, questionnaires, surveys, observations, and many more. Regardless of their particular form and nature, summary and interpretation of the data are mandatory. All performed steps used to obtain your data must be written down, such that the data can be reproduced.

My initial approaches were all based on Excel sheets with text incorporated to explain the purpose of each cell. But each time a sheet was reused, I had to look at each formula in the individual cells to understand which calculations were performed. For complex analysis, this took a lot of time and was not practical. A better option in these cases is professional statistics software such as SPSS and R. While the commercial SPSS is more convenient for Excel users due to similar user interfaces, look into code-based approaches like the freely available language R together with an editor like R-Studio; using them can be very efficient.

In code-based data analysis, you may re-use your code-lines from previous scripts, which saves a lot of time and work, as often you have a number of different analyses for each experiment. You can add commentary lines within the analysis code and thus put analysis steps and associated explanations together. While the code on its own only allows to reproduce your results, the comments may guide you and others through the document and associated analysis. Such small comments make it possible to follow an analysis workflow even years later, which the next PhD student, or a future you, might benefit from. A desirable feature of the data analysis program you use is that it can export files to common formats, such as Word, PDF, or HTML. Ideally, these export files contain not only actual results, but also analysis scripts and code comments, such that they are easily sharable with supervisors, colleagues and students.

Supervision: Traveling as Crew Members

Doing a PhD may include substantial teaching duties, and even acting as a supervisor for student projects. My own student supervision taught me that forging supervision-related content into a written form beyond simple exchange of e-mails facilitated my role with the students. Start the semester by negotiating and formulating a 'project contract' together with your students. In this contract, describe the framework of supervision, including total supervision time, mutual expectations, frequency and organization of meetings, consequences if documents are delayed, etc. The agreement can also include that each supervision meeting is preceded by a prioritized list of points to talk about, and that the students must send out minutes after each meeting. Your own doctoral supervision may require this (see Chapters 12 and 13 on supervision). A guiding question for this can be: What did we talk about? Who was assigned which task(s)? When are tasks due? Crafting meeting notes this way provides feedback for everybody and ensures that all participants know where the project is going. Share the notes on a common platform, such as Dropbox. Such a detailed plan from the very beginning allows a good estimate of the progress of the project and ensures that all comments, positive as well as negative, are clearly communicated and received.

The power of notes applies equally for your role as supervisor and supervisee—both of you are interested in an efficient way of working together. Use e-mail correspondence with your supervisor to have as much of your communication as possible in writing. A written record helps to avoid misunderstandings and might provide useful documentation if a disagreement occurs. Another important note in the relationship with your supervisor is the meeting agenda for your supervisor meetings. To make best use of the limited time for these meetings, always prepare an agenda and a list of prioritized items. Prioritizing helps when time is short to go through everything, so that you at least cover and discuss the most urgent things. Alternatively, more sophisticated prioritizing methods can be used, for example, by sorting the items in a 2 × 2 urgency-matrix, also known as an Eisenhower Matrix, to find focus (Pinola, 2012). Develop the agenda continuously by keeping a 'need to talk about' sheet on your desk. Every time something comes up that you want to discuss with your supervisor, add it to the list. Include research activities, written experimental setups, code of data analysis and such like. All that is left before the meeting is then to rank the items and send the finalized agenda to your supervisor. After the meeting, go through the minutes, make a work plan and file the meeting notes for later reference.

Conferences: Sharing with Others

At some point during your PhD project, you will start to share your research with peers at conferences. These are exciting opportunities to hear from fellow researchers and to contribute your own research. These kinds of events provide plenty of opportunities to make notes. Be prepared and have your paper and pen ready. I keep a hard copy journal just for conferences, and I prefer hand-written notes since I feel the content sinking in better during this kind of writing and journaling. You may prefer loose papers, a computer, or your tablet. Find out which approach suits you best when it comes to noting important pieces of information. If you plan to share your notes later, a digital document might be advantageous. On the other hand, hand written notes may be better suited to capture all details from information-dense presentations, including sketches and graphs. You can always image these with your phone or camera.

During presentations, focus on the main points and promising references rather than on every detail. I use a separate page for each talk and start my entries by stating the date, a short title and the name of the speaker. This is followed by the actual notes, which I write in one column with a 2 cm margin for site comments. Writing in more complex layouts did not work well for me, since it required too much of my attention and I could not focus on the actual presentation. Make a note if something in a talk catches your attention. Later on, you can contact the speaker and ask for the presented slides, which most will be very happy to share, and follow up on what caught your attention. Questions that you have during the talk can also go into your journal, and typically you get a chance to ask them immediately after the talk in the plenary question and answer session.

After a conference is finished, re-read all your notes, and mark and highlight important things with colors. Tasks that follow can include downloading interesting articles, sending e-mails to speakers you found interesting, and even asking for their slides. Once the conference notes are revisited, properly arranged and well integrated with the rest of your notes, they strengthen the power of your research.

Final Notes

Working in academia offers many opportunities to jot down thoughts and ideas. For reading, data analysis or conferencing, use notes to conserve your current thoughts, and use them later on to recover the idea. Use notes for a more concrete purpose, like when you use results from the past to design new experiments in the future or when you prepare your next supervisor meeting.

In all these situations, notes are invaluable, yet cheap—the only price to pay is the time to take the note. Whether you prefer handwriting and hard copy journals, or the electric touch, find the method that works for you—it is not the form that matters, but the content. Your notes don't need to be perfect, they just need to be useful, legible and understandable to you. Don't bother with the font type or color, as it's the information contained in the notes that counts. Always have your writing and note taking tools within reach, including besides your bed as some of the best ideas may come during sleep. The greater part of this chapter was crafted from small thoughts recorded during bed time. With each word written, with each page filled, you are one step closer to mastering the art of turning paper into power.

A Quick Toolbox

The vast amount of available software leaves you with many options and decisions to be made. Here is a list of tools worth considering when you start equipping your personal toolbox.

Tools for statistical data analysis:

- **Microsoft Excel:** Frequently used calculation program with a spreadsheet-based format (More information: https://support.office.com)
- **R and R-Studio:** The statistical programming language R and the interface R-Studio are both freely available and allow coding-based data analysis and visualization. A multitude of online tutorials explain the various features and applications of R (More information: https://cran.r-project.org and www.rstudio.com)
- **SPSS:** Commercial software for advanced statistical analysis. Intuitive application due to graphical menu selection, but coding-based approaches are also possible (More information: https://www.ibm.com/us-en/marketplace/spss-statistics)

Tools for qualitative data analysis:

- **Atlas.ti:** Commercial tool for qualitative research. Integrated tools can be used to code, visualize and explore large sets of qualitative data (More information: http://atlasti.com/)
- **HyperRESEARCH:** Commercial software for qualitative research using text, graphic, audio and video data (More information: http://www.researchware.com/)
- **Nvivo:** Commercial tool for qualitative data analysis. It allows organization and analysis of unstructured data (More information: http://www.qsrinternational.com/product/nvivo-mac)
- **QDA Miner:** Commercial software for qualitative data analysis. Features include tools for importing, visualization and statistical analysis (More information: https://provalisresearch.com/)

Tools for reference management:

- **BibDesk:** Open-source reference manager for MacOS. It contains features for import and export of citations. A search function allows to skim whole bibliographies for specific terms (More information: http://bibdesk.sourceforge.net/)
- **EndNote:** Commercial reference manager which allows to import, export and organize citation libraries. Download of references is frequently offered as EndNote-format by bibliographic databases (More information: http://endnote.com/)
- **Evernote:** Note-taking tool which is available as commercial or a free version. The website http://www.nextscientist.com/evernote-for-research-phd/ demonstrates different applications of Evernote for PhDs (More information: https://evernote.com/)
- **JabRef:** This reference manager is based on the BibTex-format and therefore complies well with LaTeX-documents (More information: http://www.jabref.org/)
- **Mendeley:** The basic version of this reference manager is free. It comes along with tools for full-text search across papers, annotating PDFs and incorporating citations in Word- and Open Office-documents (More information: https://www.mendeley.com/)
- **Zotero:** Free reference manager which offers easy ways of import, export and formatting of citations (More information: https://www.zotero.org/)

References

Cendrowski, M. (Director), Lorre, C. (Writer), & Prady, B. (Writer). (2012). The higgs boson observation [Television series episode]. In C. Lorre, S. Molaro, & B. Prady (Executive Producers), *The big bang theory*. Los Angelas, CA: Columbia Broadcasting System.

Mills, C. W. (1980). On intellectual craftsmanship (1952). *Society*, *17*(2), 63–70.

Peironcely, J. (n.d.). *7 smart ways to use Evernote for research as a PhD—Next scientist*. Retrieved from http://www.nextscientist.com/evernote-for-research-phd/

Pinola, M. (2012). *Eisenhower helps you prioritize your tasks with the urgency-importance matrix*. Retrieved from http://lifehacker.com/5942972/eisenhower-helps-you-prioritize-your-tasks-with-the-urgency-importance-matrix

Thomson, J. A. (2007). How to start–and keep–a laboratory notebook. *Intellectual Property Management in Health and Agricultural Innovation: A Handbook of Best Practices*, *8*(2), 1–9.

CHAPTER THREE

Feedback as an Integral Part of Academic Writing

ANDREAS KAMSTRUP

I rewrote the first part of A Farewell to Arms *at least fifty times. You've got to work it over. The first draft of anything is shit!* [Ernest Hemingway]

—SAMUELSON (1984)

Introduction

There is no suspenseful ending in this chapter. The message is blunt: First and foremost, write! This chapter will help you get familiar and comfortable with writing. It will demystify the process. An important part of that is finding the right people to give you feedback throughout your project. The sooner you undertake your writing and the better you are at involving the right people to give feedback, the better your dissertation or thesis will be.

My submission is mere months away, and in this last, hectic, and in many ways insecure phase, I realise success does not lay in coming up with brilliant and unique ideas, it does not lay in the dissemination of results, or even to be an expert oral communicator. While these skills are essential for doctoral study, what you will be measured on is the written work you hand in. In short, you need to be able to produce good text, and good text is achieved through good writing. During my PhD project, I have learned that sharing text is both time efficient *and* efficient in improving the quality. When the community to evaluate my text is somehow involved in the making of the text, the text will develop further than if done in solitude.

Unfortunately, the PhD project is often experienced as a solitary process without camaraderie and only a supervisor to engage with. Other writing 'communities' are most often either specific research environments or unknown journal editors and reviewers. This latter kind of long-range feedback is very important as it affords the author a break-away from the text and then a later revisit with keen eyes and new angles. However, the kind of feedback this chapter will focus on is a more immediate type of feedback. Feedback that more actively forms and influences the writing process.

This chapter will show how I found or created four different occasions for feedback that greatly enhanced the quality of my writing. These four occasions include a PhD course on flow writing, a feedback seminar, forming a feedback group and co-writing with a senior colleague. Some of these occasions were already existing and my effort merely consisted in signing up; others demanded a more active effort where I was involved in creating them.

During my doctorial research, I have travelled to many universities, participating in both PhD seminars at other universities, pre-conference workshops and longer research stays in both Europe and the US. This has made it clear that Denmark (and possibly also the rest of the Nordic countries) has a very particular understanding of the PhD role in regards to (academic) independency. For instance, when I visited Stanford University, the PhD group there was much closer to their supervisor, receiving feedback on various topics in a much more detailed manner. In Denmark, the PhD student is more 'on his/her own', which can be both negative and positive. The following four occasions for feedback is a product of an environment where the PhD student is expected to actively create and structure the context of the doctoral research.

Let Your Writing Flow with 'Flow Writing'

In Denmark, PhD courses are a mandatory part of completing a PhD. These courses can be either research specific (protein chemistry, reading Aristotle through Heidegger, etc.) or more generic (getting research into journals, media training for researchers, etc.). I took advantage of a generic course on *flow writing*, which is a writing approach primarily based on Csikszentmihalyi's (1996) theory of flow and Boice's (1992) research in academic writing. As your program may not offer such a course, the description below is also offered as a 'how to'. There is no reason you cannot use the technique in the privacy of your own office.

The technique does not require any prerequisites. It is a simple matter of typing continuously, and thereby creating text. Besides continuously writing (at all time you have to type letters even if it seems meaningless), the only other rule is that you cannot look at the screen while doing it. An important guiding principle is that if you have an idea that you wish to write about, try approaching it actively. For instance, write *I find it hard to analyse the experimental data in regards to the theory of general relativity, because the theory does not take into account the …* By doing this you put words on paper about a difficult concept or idea, which you can then refine and elaborate, and at some point, invite others to help you with. Part of the argument in flow writing is also, that merely writing it down will help to resolve these difficulties or blocks.

A good way to start this exercise is to write for 10 minutes about your main research question to warm up, then have a small break and come back and write about more specific ideas for a paper or a chapter. After 10 minutes of typing, you should end up with somewhere between one and three pages. As you'll find, flow writing can be a very powerful tool for jump-starting a writing process, as it forces the writer to create a (very rough) first draft of a paper, which can then be refined and revised. When flow-writing with a fellow PhD student or other colleague, after writing for 10-minutes, spend a couple of minutes reading through what you wrote, giving it a *very brief* brush up by removing the most distracting elements (like grammatical errors, typos, and so forth). Because the text is conceived as it is, the expectations in regards to coherence, progress, and strength of argument will be smaller. The focus of feedback here is more about ideas and understanding. Flow writing with a colleague emphasises the value of receiving feedback before a text becomes more developed.

The flow writing process illustrates how early in a process text can be circulated for feedback. It was productive for me to think about not when a paper is good in absolute terms, but when it is *good enough to circulate.* Flow writing is a technique that can be practiced almost without specific resources, and is an embodiment of a famed slogan which is powerful in its simplicity: *Just do it!*

Feedback Seminars

At my department, there is an annual two-day get-together for all scientific staff. Participation is mandatory for permanent staff, but voluntary for PhD students. At this seminar, every participant presents work-in-progress, that is, a paper not yet finished. The presentation can be ideas for a conference paper, thoughts for a full paper, book proposals, programme ideas, or tentative research findings. In outlining a feedback seminar, you will not only see the benefit of the practice, but also get ideas for encouraging similar seminars in your department or study group.

The seminar has ground rules to optimize the best possible feedback (Caffarella & Barnett, 2000). First of all, every paper is assigned to two dedicated readers, where at least one is senior. Secondly, there is a strict time frame: the feedback is opened as a discussion between the two dedicated readers, where they present their take on the paper's main idea, structure, methods, strengths, weaknesses and possible future directions. This is scheduled to last 20 minutes. For the last part of the discussion (also 20 minutes) the floor is opened to include everyone, including the author, in the discussion. It is very important to have and abide to these ground rules as they help to secure a dedicated read and feedback of all papers, no matter how elaborate and well-developed they are. Feedback—when it is well delivered—is not about a text being *good* or *bad*, but rather about how to *improve* the text. Because the feedback seminars are structured to begin with a dialogue between two discussants (and not the author), the feedback can develop in surprising and unforeseen directions.

If your department does not already organize such feedback seminars, there is no reason that you—in collaboration with senior colleagues—cannot suggest it to the head of the department. If the practice is not embraced at department level, form a PhD feedback group (as I and a couple of other PhD students did at my department) and incorporate the practice of the feedback seminar into your group activities.

Forming a Feedback Group

At my PhD school, two students arranged a seminar. At the end of this seminar, we wanted to stay in touch, having a meeting approximately once a month. Eventually these meetings solidified as a *feedback group*, which was distinct from a reading group: the focus was on giving and receiving feedback. In this group (of five PhD students), we were very specific on determining ground rules, that is, we organized and elaborated on how we should interact and give feedback. We were keen to enforce these rules, which for us was quite different from other reading groups we had participated in. Our experience from more traditional reading groups is that these have a more unstructured and loosely defined engagement with the circulated text.

Establishing ground rules for running a feedback group is important. In my feedback group, it was agreed that a small reading guide should be enclosed when the paper for discussion was circulated. In a reading guide, the author can indicate which sections or themes to focus on. As the feedback was between peers (PhD to

PhD) this clarification was necessary, since we as students did not have the same overview as more experienced scholars—we needed help with how to structure and give relevant feedback in ways the professors at the feedback seminar were quite experienced in. The reading guide helped us to focus on what the writer wanted feedback on. Another ground rule was that comments should always focus on pushing the text forward—we were not allowed to criticize without also suggesting an alternative.

Of course, it is a good idea to sometimes allow for some broad and unasked-for feedback, since this can potentially present radical new ideas that can move the text and the argument to unexpected places. If you do not specify, at least in broad terms, what you would like the feedback givers to focus on, you can end up getting diverse and unfocused feedback that becomes very difficult to use. If you want to keep a door open for other forms of feedback, structure the session so that only a fraction of the time is spent on this and the majority is spent on what you feel you need feedback on.

Being good at giving feedback strengthens the capacity for receiving and incorporating feedback. Similarly, focusing on how to give feedback sharpens your idea about how you want feedback, as it trains you to think about text as a *process*. Feedback skills can be mastered and improved through practice. In the feedback group, we not only got feedback, but continuously learned to give it. A feedback group of doctoral students also allows for the freedom to present what may seem half-baked arguments and open, unfinished texts, without being apologetic and shameful about it (Aitchison, 2009; Cameron, Nairn, & Higgins, 2009).

Co-writing a Paper with a Senior Colleague

In the examples above, the phases of writing and receiving feedback are with unfinished texts. Co-writing a finished paper with a more experienced writer is also invaluable in developing writing and editing skills. The feedback in this exercise will be from a more experienced writer.

I recall how I went for coffee in the department kitchen one afternoon and two hours later I had co-developed an idea for a paper, which I and a senior colleague were to write together. Waiting for the coffee to brew, an assistant professor arrived and we got to talking. It turned out we had been studying the same phenomenon from different angles and we agreed that we should see if we could write something together. Drawing on techniques learned in flow writing, I produced a (by no means brilliant) extended abstract, which I sent to him.

Co-writing can mean many things across disciplines. In the natural sciences, there is strong tradition of writing group-based papers, while in some branches of the humanities solo writing is more common. In my field (sociology of work and organization theory), there is no overarching tradition in the sense that both writing alone or in smaller groups is normal. Also in my field, there is no taxonomy in authorship and no built-in understanding of being either first, second or last author.

Co-writing (when accomplished as actual writing text together) can be rather intense. Our co-writing mostly took place in our own offices, as we shared work online using a shared drive. We used Microsoft Word and in particular the *Comments* and *Track Changes* functionality. Adding a comment will produce a small box in the margin where suggestions, questions, or elaboration can be written. *Track changes* is a feature that will underline all additions and strike-through suggested deletions, so that they are still viewable in the document. With these two functions, it is possible to give direct and close-to-text feedback. Tossing the paper back and forth a couple of times a week with someone who had the same stake in it was both a demanding and a rewarding process. Disagreements about formulations or how to frame the argument had to be dealt with upfront; working with someone who cared as much about the text as I did taught me that if I wanted my formulations and my ideas to prevail I had to produce strong and clear arguments. As the ambition was to submit the paper to a particular conference, we had a specific deadline, which worked to encourage timely effort.

Actual co-writing includes concrete and direct feedback, and can entail almost day-to-day feedback on small chunks of work, from one or two paragraphs, to entire sections. Receiving and giving feedback in this manner benefits from actuality—you receive feedback on something you have just worked on. This is often not the case when you submit a paper for review by a journal, as feedback in that case can take months. When co-writing with a colleague the feedback is prompt, timely and fresh.

My flow written abstract eventually developed into a conference paper, which we presented together. Additional feedback from the conference was worked into the paper, we made some recommended changes and now it is published as a book chapter.

Feedback Roles

Working in a structured manner with feedback, you may discover that it can be fruitful to arrange the type of feedback you are looking for in different categories. Similar in form to the Six Thinking Hats developed by De Bono (1999), where each member of a discussion group takes on specific roles (emotional, factual, cautious, creative, and the like), feedback roles can give a lens to focus your groups review. Below are the roles I encourage to those I work with in feedback groups:

- *The encouraging*: focuses on what works and how to develop this even further
- *The practical*: focuses on flow of language, grammar and meaningfulness
- *The scientific*: focuses on the strength of the argument and internal coherence
- *The outsider*: plays the role of the ignorant conversation partner
- *The provocateur*: is the devil's advocate and challenges premises
- *The expert*: focuses on the contribution of the text and which journal to aim for
- *The gatekeeper*: is a strategic reader who can open doors and present new possibilities

These roles are not always in play, but they serve as a constant reminder that feedback unfolds in many ways.

Conclusion

Writing is a continuous process that continues through the entire PhD project. When seeking to create occasions for feedback, the scope of deadlines can be transformed from something intimidating into something productive. Although writing is more often a private matter developing quality text has a public side to it, such as with feedback (Maher et al., 2008). It is key to learn how to receive feedback, to learn how to incorporate relevant advice and to determine which feedback is most relevant to your needs. Feedback is a craft and a skill that is improved through working with it and reflecting upon it.

References

Aitchison, C. (2009). Writing groups for doctoral education. *Studies in Higher Education, 34*(8), 905–916.

Boice, R. (1992). *The new faculty member: Supporting and fostering professional development.* San Francisco, CA: Jossey-Bass.

Caffarella, R. S., & Barnett, B. G. (2000). Teaching doctoral students to become scholarly writers: The importance of giving and receiving critiques. *Studies in Higher Education, 25*(1), 39–52.

Cameron, J., Nairn, K., & Higgins, J. (2009). Demystifying academic writing: Reflections on emotions, know-how and academic identity. *Journal of Geography in Higher Education, 33*(2), 269–284.

Csikszentmihalyi, M. (1996). *Flow and the psychology of discovery and invention*. New York, NY: Harper Collins.
De Bono, E. (1999). *Six thinking hats* (Vol. 192). New York, NY: Back Bay Books.
Maher, D., Seaton, L., McMullen, C., Fitzgerald, T., Otsuji, E., & Lee, A. (2008). 'Becoming and being writers': The experiences of doctoral students in writing groups. *Studies in Continuing Education, 30*(3), 263–275.
Samuelson, A. (1984). *With Hemingway: A year in Key West and Cuba*. New York, NY: Random House.

CHAPTER FOUR

Failures and Setbacks

Contaminated Cell Cultures, Missing Data and Rejected Manuscripts

ROOPE A. KALLIONPÄÄ

Introduction

Failures and setbacks are an integral and inevitable part of research. Failures and setbacks are the various disappointing surprises, problems and obstacles that you may face during doctoral studies. Some of them are related to your decisions and actions, while others happen irrespective of your choices. If you work in a laboratory, you will have surely experienced the variety of ways things can go wrong: cell culture contamination, experiments yielding inconsistent results or machines breaking down. Those involved in clinical or social research may encounter difficulties in patient recruiting, unmotivated participants and drop-outs of the research study altogether. Surveys and registers may suffer from missing or biased data, and statistical models may fail to converge. Printers get stuck, files are corrupted and important papers are lost, typically at the worst possible moment. Even the peer review system and unsuccessful funding applications can steadily produce disappointments. Is any of this starting to sound familiar to you?

When I started my PhD project in cancer research three years ago, I spent the first month trying to extract DNA with reagents (a substance or mixture for use in chemical analysis or other reactions) expired long ago, and I now know to avoid this kind of mistake. Although increasing experience will help foreseeing and avoiding many of the potential pitfalls, setbacks are always part of research, and learning to cope with them is a major aspect of doctoral studies.

This chapter will discuss strategies for staying positive amidst problems, prioritization of your values, maintaining a balance between different projects and other areas of your life, tracking your process in log books and openly discussing failures with others. I share examples of my own experience as a researcher within molecular cancer research and disease epidemiology in Finland, but the lessons are not restricted to a specific field. Failures and setbacks appear regardless of methodology.

Do Not Blame Yourself

One of the most vital strategies for coping with research-related problems is remembering that science, even social science, is inherently a business of trial and error. Disappointments, difficulties and setbacks are part of the process and failures can be much more common in research than in everyday life. This is both because of the complex and sensitive methods in use, and the nature of research as a work with the unknown. Most scientific failures cannot be evaded even with the best efforts and preparations. You need to accept this feature of research and give up on the idea of perfectionism. You may easily end up blaming yourself for your problems, but you should actively remind yourself that they are not automatically your fault.

Dissect the failure and the actions leading to it. Finding out the immediate reason, such as some inappropriate experimental parameter, is the standard practice, yet it is worth going a bit further and considering how you ended up to choose that specific parameter value. There are three possible outcomes: First, if you had no means to know better, you have successfully demonstrated that the failure was not because of you. Second, if you could have made a better choice, you have now learned how to adjust your planning process, and the future likelihood of a similar failure decreases. And third, if even finding out what actually went wrong turns out to be difficult, you surely could not have predicted the problem. Therefore, it does not matter if you fail, and you just need the persistence to try again.

Prioritize Your Values

I often find myself rushing from one deadline to another, desperately trying to get everything done. Doctoral studies are full of things to do: the research itself, laboratory housekeeping, teaching and studying, reading and writing. You may easily drift between urgent tasks unless you specifically take the time to prioritize. Your 'to do' list will need to be prioritized regularly, yet you should also consider broader topics and your own values. Without actively reflecting on what you value the most and which things are of the highest importance, you may end up acting in ways which neglect the aspects of your life that matter the most. For many of us, values like family first, good health and happiness are high up in the list, yet we still neglect our loved ones, eat unhealthy food and give up physical exercise because of the pressing needs at work or during our studies. If you spend all your time studying and doing research, and they end up taking a disproportionately large part of your life, failures grow larger. In contrast, if your days contain activities other than the research, such as playing football or time spent with friends and family, a disastrous day at the laboratory or in the field does not mean that the whole day would be ruined. In research, it is often wise to try different approaches in parallel to minimize the effects of a failure in one line. Similarly, it is good to build your everyday life around many activities, so that a bad day, week or month without progress in studies or research does not leave you feeling that absolutely nothing good has happened.

When you have considered your values and goals to identify the ones most important to you, it is easier to make decisions in line with them instead of just trying to get through the most urgent issues. Good prioritization increases your efficiency, but it also helps to build resiliency. Does the failure actually matter? Do you really need to succeed with this experiment? Is it important in the scale of your life? Is it worth worrying about?

When you are sad because of a setback, hearing these questions may feel annoying. However, having thought about your priorities beforehand, it may be easier to at least forget the problems once the working day ends.

See the Big Picture

Always aim at maintaining a general view of your thesis project. This involves having goals, a plan for reaching those goals and also knowing what has already been accomplished so far. It is very easy to go off on other tangents without bringing yourself back to your research plan. Despite the required extra effort, you should frequently go back to your earlier results, and even tabulate them to clarify what you have already done—you may have more data than you thought.

Focusing on the big picture also helps you to coordinate your next actions efficiently. Even more important, it keeps up motivation and promotes a positive frame of mind. Keeping your research goals at the front of your mind reminds you why you are doing each experiment and what might be achieved. Observing the data and results piling up is motivating and encouraging as it makes your progress visible before writing up the results.

Think about the even bigger picture, dream of high impact publications, the time after finishing your thesis or even a future professorship. Even if such dreams do not seem realistic at the moment, they show you a forward direction and provide motivation to keep moving forward and progressing your research.

Small Baskets

Since failures and problems are inevitable, it is often wise to avoid putting all your eggs in one basket. This means having a few projects running in parallel, as long as the number is quite small and you are still able to adequately concentrate on each project. For example, cell culture experiments may be accompanied by tissue analysis or even epidemiological work. Too many projects will only cause stress and failures stemming from excessive hurry, so each project should be of a manageable size.

Running parallel projects increases the likelihood of having some successes even though you may be stuck with one line of research. This ensures the progress of your studies, relieving the stress and pressures. Experiencing successes in one project also facilitates maintaining a positive attitude and building resiliency when encountering failures in another project. You may find useful crosstalk between the projects, and advances in one area may solve problems from the neighboring project. For example, I set up a statistical method to analyze epidemiological data and later applied the same approach to results from cell culture experiments.

Remember that Some Questions are More Difficult than Others

Some research projects seem to proceed more smoothly than others, but you should never compare your progress with that of others. You have your own research questions and the effort and the number of attempts needed to find the answers are specific to these questions and cannot be compared with other projects. The differences may be due to a variety of reasons, as some research questions are more complex than others, and sometimes more preliminary work and preparations are needed. When your project requires trial and error, the question addressed is likely to be difficult enough. If everything was clear at the beginning, you probably were not working with something truly novel.

Some questions are too difficult, no matter how hard you push on them. This may be due to an insufficient number of subjects or the lack of suitable methods to measure the phenomenon of interest. If you have data on one million people and wish to study something with prevalence around one in ten million, no statistical manipulation will allow you to get robust results. In such cases, you just need to accept the facts and move on. Having invested a lot of time and effort on a project that turns out to be impossible is definitely a major setback. However, the decision to discontinue an excessively difficult project may be a relief: no more time and energy are wasted.

List Your Worries and Develop Backup Plans

After a day full of problems, I usually start developing backup plans. I may not even know yet if anything actually went wrong, but it is reassuring to have some idea of the potential next steps. For example, if a statistical model fails to converge, I list potential transformations that could be applied to the data. If I feel uncertain whether I added some reagent to a laboratory experiment, I try to come up with ways to test its presence afterwards.

If you feel distressed, it may be a good idea to write a list of all your problems and try to come up with the first steps of finding solutions. Even if none of the resulting ideas are doable in the end, writing down the list helps you to get your worries in some sort of perspective. When you come back to the list, you may have completely new ideas or refinements to your earlier plans.

Get Back to Your Notebooks

When a study is published, you may wonder why it took so long to find the solutions that now seem so self-evident. Why did I write tons of code when there is a ready-made function to do the same thing better? Why was I not recording that key characteristic of my experiments from the beginning? Why did I try to discover something that I later found to have been published already a decade ago?

I am often annoyed by the time spent in all these detours, since in hindsight it is easy to draw the line from the first idea to the final results. However, during the process even the goal may be vague, let alone the path leading there. Traveling all the twists is needed to discover the route, and there is no need to worry about these curves. They are part of the process, and the path was not obvious to anyone before you went through it. To demonstrate this, it is a good idea to track the project in your laboratory journals or other notes. Having some type of diary or log book for this purpose is worthwhile even if you do not work in a laboratory, such as a qualitative researchers field notes. Reading old notes usually shows that you could not have changed anything to reach your goal faster. If you manage to spot some recurrent pattern of situations where different actions could have been a better choice, use this information to avoid similar delays in future projects. For this purpose, writing down the reasons and justifications of all the choices, experiments and ideas is highly recommendable when making notes.

Do Not Lose Your Hope in the Publishing Process

You will inevitably encounter setbacks when trying to publish your work. This may mean nasty comments from reviewers or negative editorial decisions. Although reviewer comments are mainly unbiased and based on the actual work, this may not always be the case. When reading the decision letters and comments, you should always remember that they may be influenced by personal opinions or interests. One reviewer may consider a manuscript the best one ever, while another reviewer judges it too bad for even providing any specific comments. Never take reviewer comments personally or lose your hope with a manuscript critiqued by a reviewer. When you do not let yourself sink into despair, it is easier to utilize the comments and feedback to make your manuscript even better. I typically have an ordered list of other potential journals when I am submitting a manuscript for peer review. That way a rejection does not feel as much like a problem, since I can just move on to the next step of the plan. The feedback from that 'rejection' can even make the contribution stronger.

Negative results or findings that contradict earlier publications are a common problem in publishing, yet they should not be a reason to worry. The negative or unexpected results advance science and should definitely be published. Getting such results does not equal a delay in finishing your thesis. Luckily, many journals are starting to recognize the importance of publishing negative results to avoid enforcing publication bias that results from the lower likelihood of negative results being published. In the case of negative results, (for example, the lack of an association between two conditions) you just need look for a journal that is committed to publishing negative findings.

Results that contradict earlier research are part of the scientific process that ultimately leads to a consensus that is more likely resembling 'the truth'. There are typically plenty of differences in the design and methods between contradicting studies and these differences are probably accountable for the disagreement. There is not necessarily anything wrong with your work. Take the time to read the earlier studies in detail and point out the most likely reasons for the discrepancies, and you do not need to worry anymore.

Publishing negative or unexpected findings may require more effort, but at least you can feel content for having reduced bias in the scientific literature.

Utilize the Failures for Learning and Discovery

Setbacks are seldom without value, and sometimes they may even yield valuable insights. There is no need to repeat the story of the 'accidental' discovery of penicillin, where a Petri dish accidentally left out showed inhibited bacteria growth. Failed experiments and accidents may reveal something you did not even ask, even if they did not yield new antibiotics. Being watchful for unexpected discoveries is necessary in the cases of both failed and successful experiments. The chance of surprising discoveries can motivate you to stay positive during the research.

Even if you did not know it at the moment, you may later need information from your previous failed experiments—it may be, for example, the role of some reagent you once forgot to add or the effect of a different temperature. Finding out which approaches are useless at least narrows down the set of possible ways to go. Recently, a research group from Haverford College published a method for discovering novel inorganic-organic hybrid materials (Raccuglia et al., 2016). The method utilizes data from failed experiments collected from laboratory notebooks and outperforms experienced human chemists, demonstrating that what seems like failures may actually represent a significant resource of information.

Of course, most of the time failures yield no fundamental scientific insights or groundbreaking results. Nevertheless, they offer a great chance for personal learning. Contamination in cell culture means an opportunity to develop your aseptic technique. Crashing computer shoing the value of frequent back-ups. Negative referee comments show which aspects of a manuscript require special attention. A major part of doctoral studies is getting experience in conducting research. Quite often, this means trial and error—learning how to do things, what to do and what to avoid. Failures and setbacks are likely to have some value even though you never wish to experience problems. Consider them as chances for novel discoveries and learning.

Share Your Difficulties

Our upbringing and school education favor avoiding failures, and when they occur, hiding them. As a result, we are often ashamed of our failures and try to hide or downplay them (Vallery, 2016). This should not be the way to go in research. Failed experiments are often scientifically interesting or important and should therefore be openly discussed within the research group. Keeping all the problems to yourself is extremely hard and wearing—especially so, if you try to hide them from your supervisor or peers.

Discussing problems with others also brings other benefits. Talking about your difficulties with someone else, such as your supervisors and peers, forces you to formulate the problem more clearly and may help to find the answer. Those who are not deeply involved in your research can often be better at thinking outside the box and make useful suggestions, be it anything from using smaller gloves (Vallery, 2016) to a different method for fitting your statistical models.

By sharing your failures, you help others to avoid the same pitfalls. You can foster an atmosphere permissive for discussing setbacks by being open about your own problems. You also get to benefit from the problems others have faced without running into the same troubles yourself.

Be Aware of Your Mood and Put Health First

The risks of injury, illness or death are not an acceptable part of modern research. While it is clear that all actions to prevent accidents in the laboratory setting need to be taken, you should also remember to take care of your mental health. If you always feel depressed, anxious or exhausted, it may be wise to seek for help or to reduce the workload. If research absorbs all joy from your life and leaves you exhausted and depressed, quitting or postponing your science is an option to consider. Health, both physical and mental, is more important than finishing a PhD.

Failures may cause significant stress and anxiety during graduate school. Up to 73.6% of graduate students have been reported to feel stressed or very stressed (Oswalt & Riddock, 2007), while another study has found that 76.9% of graduate students felt exhausted and 27.2% depressed in the last 12 months (Wyatt & Oswalt, 2013). This is related to the many pressures of postgraduate studies: responsibility and independence, multitasking with teaching and research, uncertainty of funding, and the urge to produce results to progress in the studies. The last aspect causes stress especially when things do not go as expected—it often feels as if the more you experience setbacks, the later you will finish your thesis.

Deepening melancholy may lead to a depressive disorder that is a medical condition and should be treated appropriately. The strategies outlined in this chapter may help to avoid a negative frame of mind, but the actual depressive disorder requires medical attention. Mental health issues in postgraduate studies are the subject of Chapter 9 in this book.

Conclusion

Difficulties, disappointments and setbacks can be an inherent part of research. Recognizing and accepting this aspect of research is important to minimize stress and anxiety. Key elements in maintaining a positive attitude include prioritization of your values, maintaining a balance between different projects and other areas of life, tracking your process in log books and openly discussing failures with others. Setbacks and failures are not without value, they are chances for learning and discovery.

References

Oswalt, S. B., & Riddock, C. C. (2007). What to do about being overwhelmed: Graduate students, stress and university services. *The College Student Affairs Journal, 27*(1), 24–44.

Raccuglia, P., Elbert, K. C., Adler, P. D. F., Falk, C., Wenny, M. B., Mollo, A., … Norquist, A. J. (2016). Machine-learning-assisted materials discovery using failed experiments. *Nature, 533*(7601), 73–77.

Vallery, T. K. (2016). Growth from failure. *Science, 353*(6298), 514.

Wyatt, T., & Oswalt, S. B. (2013). Comparing mental health issues among undergraduate and graduate students. *American Journal of Health Education, 44*(2), 96–107.

CHAPTER FIVE

Writing the PhD Thesis

Planning, Getting Started and Getting Done

JAKOB ROSENKRANTZ DE LASSON

Introduction

The process of writing the PhD thesis is surrounded by a mythical aura. From senior colleagues, you may have heard that it is a long and tough process, in which you will be all on your own against the ticking watch of the deadline. For a good part of my PhD project, I dreaded writing the thesis. But as I was approaching the write up phase, an older colleague reminded me that I'll only ever write one PhD thesis, and that I shouldn't forget to *enjoy* the writing process. Enjoying the process is not a goal in its own right, but is an important means to reach your goal, because you'll write a better thesis if you enjoy the process.

Enjoying writing your PhD thesis is not something you decide, and then it magically happens. Enjoying the writing will happen if you understand the process, get an overview of it, and understand the psychology of why it can be difficult to write. In this chapter, I demystify the PhD writing process (Single, 2009) by breaking it into smaller and more manageable pieces. I propose a three-step procedure to *plan*, *get started*, and *get done* with your thesis writing. Each step has its own key objectives. To plan, you must get an overview of your thesis. To get started, you must build writing momentum and use it to produce text. To get done, you must make your text coherent and tidy it up. This chapter offers practical measures to reach these key objectives.

Planning

> *A goal without a plan is just a wish.* [Antoine de Saint-Exupéry]
>
> —Koenig & Schultz (2010, p. 250)

As with any big task or project, planning is essential. Well before you need to start the actual writing, *plan* the writing. This investment in time will make the writing process more enjoyable and the final outcome, your PhD thesis, more coherent. So, while it can be tempting to spend the couple of days that this planning will take on tangible research work, I urge you to resist; you'll be rewarded accordingly.

How Long Will Writing Your Thesis Take?

Assessing the time required to write your thesis is an important part of planning the thesis writing. However, it is also a question that cannot be answered simply, as the answer will depend on a number of factors that are specific for your PhD project. The length of the PhD project plays a role. In Denmark, where I did my PhD, the length of a PhD project is almost always exactly three years, and it is hard to imagine spending more than six months of this relatively short project period on thesis writing. In Sweden, as a comparison, a PhD project takes at least four years, which potentially leaves more time for thesis writing.

The type of thesis that you decide to write also influences the time you need to write it. There are essentially two kinds of theses: A monograph or an article thesis. The monograph is a longer and more in-depth form of the thesis, in which you present your research and elaborate on findings and results. As opposed to this longer form of the thesis, an article thesis is a long introduction of the research topic with all your publications appended. A monograph will take longer to write than an article-based thesis. Your number of publications might also play a role; it may be easier and less time-consuming to build a thesis around already prepared and published data, analysis, figures and conclusions.

A practical way to estimate how much time you will need for your writing is to talk to previous PhD students and ask about their experiences. As I was approaching my own thesis writing, I talked to a colleague who recently submitted his PhD thesis on a similar topic to mine. He had set aside two months for thesis writing, which he felt had been too little. After listening to him, I decided that I would need three months to write my thesis and started three and a half months before the submission deadline, to allow time for any necessary research work during the writing period. That means I allocated just below 10% of my total PhD project period for thesis writing.

Mind Map Your Project and Research

Having estimated the time needed to write it, start getting more concrete in the planning. An important first step is to get an overview of what research topics you have worked on. You most likely have a pretty good idea of this, even without writing anything down. But before drafting the table of contents, it can be useful to get a *visual* overview of your research and project.

A practical approach to visualize all your work and research is to create a mind map. Pull out a blank piece of paper—or use one of the many online mind mapping tools—and write a tentative *title for your thesis* in a big box in the middle. Think of all the *bigger topics* that you have worked on as part of your PhD and write them, using another color, in boxes around the title box. Next, think of *smaller topics* and write them with yet another color in boxes a bit further out in your mind map. Finally, list all *your publications*—journal papers, conference contributions and publication material in preparation—in boxes with a final color.

This will give you an overview of all topics in your project. What is missing are the *connections* among all these components. Draw lines between all the boxes that are, one way or the other, connected. Certain smaller topics that relate to at least one of the bigger topics can be connected to the associated bigger topic box. A given publication may be related to certain bigger and/or smaller topics and can be connected accordingly, and so forth.

I found that an online mind mapping tool, where I could easily move around and re-name boxes, was better than a piece of paper for setting up a useful map. I started making a mind map for my PhD project about three months before starting to write (six months before submission deadline). As I got closer to the starting date of my thesis writing, I took out the mind map, discussed it with my supervisors and made a final iteration of it. Discussing it with my supervisors revealed that a final component was needed before the thesis planning was over: A draft for the table of contents.

Draft the Skeleton of Your Thesis: A First Go at the Table of Contents

A good way to get started is to set up a template in the software you plan to use for writing your thesis. Look at your mind map and start drafting the chapter titles. You will most likely start and end with a type of an introduction and conclusion chapter. For all the in-between chapters, focus on the bigger topics in your mind map. These may not all become chapter titles, but can at least provide inspiration for which chapters you should include in this first draft. Finally, look at the smaller topics in your mind map and create sections in the relevant chapters.

In setting up the chapter structure of your thesis, think about the following overall flow: Introduction—Methods—Investigations and Results—Conclusions and Outlook. In my PhD thesis, I initially had two introductory chapters, then two method chapters, then five investigation and result chapters and finally a conclusion and outlook chapter.

Remember that it is a *draft*, and you can change it, such as by renaming chapters and sections and re-arranging them as your writing progresses. The important thing is that this draft is concrete in the sense that you can look at it and decide where to start writing.

Getting Started

> *Inspiration usually comes during work, rather than before it.* [Madeleine L'Engle]
> —L'ENGLE (1984, P. 143)

> *Godt begyndt er halvt fuldendt.* [Danish proverb for, 'A good start is half the work']

When you have a blank document before your eyes, it can be difficult to write anything. When you have already written something, you have a certain *writing momentum*, and writing the next sentence, and the next paragraph, and the next section goes more easily than when you have to write those first words

The most important aspect of getting started is to *build up writing momentum.* Once you have writing momentum and are able to maintain it day after day, you will produce text for your thesis and eventually finish. If you do not have momentum, the thesis writing process can be frustrating and stressful. The following suggestions all aim at helping you to build up writing momentum.

Start with the Easy Chapters

A first thing to decide when starting the writing is what chapter to start with. With a draft for your table of contents, you will have an overview of what options you have, and your choice should be motivated by your wish to build writing momentum. Start with a chapter that will be *easy* to write.

The introductory chapter, in which you will frame your research into a broader context and motivate your work, may not be easy to start with when you have not written the bulk of the thesis. Many people choose to write this chapter last. Similarly, a chapter on any work in progress may not be easy to start with. Such chapters may have loose ends, and the work could develop during the writing process, which makes it challenging to start writing when you just start your thesis writing.

In contrast, a chapter on work that you have already finished, and maybe even published, will be much easier to start with. You will have all results or data, and you will have performed the analysis and drawn conclusions—all of which can more or less directly be entered into your thesis chapter.

I started my own thesis writing with such a chapter, which was chapter nine of my ten-chapter thesis. It was work that I had done together with colleagues in the first half of my PhD, and that had been published by that point. I used a selection of figures from the publications and built the chapter around these and associated conclusions.

When you have chosen a chapter to start writing, decide which part of the chapter to start with. You can start with the easy parts, for example, describing the methods and results, which can be done more or less mechanically. If the work has already been published, interpretation and conclusions may also be fairly easy to write. Finally, write the introduction of the chapter.

Full Speed on Writing in the Morning

Start writing first thing in the morning. This is particularly easy if the day before you have made a plan for what to write on the next day. With a plan, the barrier to getting started will be reduced. Continue until lunch time if you can, and only take a few short breaks, such as whenever you finish a section. Before going to lunch, review what you have written and be happy about the actual writing that you have managed to get done.

In the afternoon, you can continue the writing, but the advantage of writing efficiently in the morning is that you will have produced most of the text you need on a given day. Writing in the afternoon will then be an option that you can use, or not. Be satisfied with having written what you needed for that day during your morning session, congratulate yourself on a job well done, and spend the rest of the day on other tasks. Before you go home, plan the next day's writing.

Write, Edit, Write, Edit, Write, Edit …

A big obstacle to building up writing momentum is the fear that the text won't be good enough. This way of thinking comes from the misconception that a piece of work, such as your text, should be *perfect*. You should, as Pettis and Stark (2017) advise, laugh at perfection as it keeps you from being done. Your text will never be perfect, but it can, upon several iterations, become *very good*.

Instead of thinking more about how to improve the first version of your text, just keep writing. Produce actual text. Do not re-read every sentence when you have written it and try to make it perfect. The time for such editing will come, but at this point, focus on writing. Just continue to write, and then re-read the text when you have finished a paragraph or a section. It is substantially easier to edit and improve an existing text than to write, on the first attempt, the final version of the text.

Print Your Thesis Draft: Feel the Weight of Your Work

While writing it is easy to focus on all the chapters and parts that lie ahead of you, which can be a drain on your writing momentum. Therefore, remind yourself of the progress you are making.

One very effective way to do this is to print your thesis draft every now and then. I would print my entire thesis draft whenever I finished the draft of another chapter. I could feel the weight of my work, which motivated me to continue writing, add more chapters and thus more weight. Additionally, the printouts were useful to bring to meetings with my supervisors for discussing my thesis writing.

Eventually these printouts will become so heavy, that you realize you are no longer getting *started* writing your PhD thesis. It has become time to getting *done.*

Getting Done

> *Kill your darlings, kill your darlings, even when it breaks your egocentric little scribbler's heart, kill your darlings.* [Stephen King]
>
> —KING (2000)

In this final phase, you no longer produce a lot of text, but instead focus on writing whatever small bits are missing and editing all that you have written to sharpen your arguments and make your thesis coherent.

Write Shorter and More Focused Chapters

As the submission deadline approaches, you may feel that you have spent too much time writing too few chapters. You may worry that you won't manage to finish the remaining chapters on time. This is deadline pressure which you can use to your advantage by writing shorter and more focused chapters.

As I had been writing for two and a half out of the three and a half months I had allocated, I had finished four out of ten chapter drafts. I was compelled to skip some of the remaining chapters, especially the ones that were not key chapters in my thesis, to be able to finish on schedule. I discussed this with my supervisors who, fortunately, convinced me that there was an alternative path: writing the remaining chapters faster and in a more focused manner. If this happens to you, you should spend fewer days per chapter at this point than in the initial phase. This *is* possible, because in writing the first part of your thesis you have developed a method and a flow for writing new chapters. You know where to start, what to write next, and where to finish the chapter. Therefore, you can apply this knowledge and experience and finish the final chapters quickly.

One reason that certain chapters might still remain to be written late in the writing process is that they contain work in progress and loose ends. This is not a problem. What you report in your PhD thesis is the work that you have done. It is natural to have loose ends and you simply have to explain this. Explain what you have done and found, and what the next steps will or would be. Then you have done the duty of reporting your research, and the next PhD student interested in the same topic or research questions can pick up from there.

Make Your Text Coherent

Take a step back and look at the entire thesis. Your text is probably not really a thesis, but rather a collection of chapters that are not coherently tied together. Therefore, it is crucial that you set aside time to read everything you have written up until now, to tie together the chapters and ensure coherency.

This is not proofreading, so do not focus on individual sentences. Instead, ask yourself if the order of your chapters is right, and if one chapter leads naturally on to the next one. Also, make sure that concepts are not introduced multiple times, but only when they first appear, and tweak your chapter and section titles. Many people are going to browse through your table of contents, while fewer are going to read your thesis. So, make sure that chapter and section titles communicate what you want people to retain about your PhD research.

Reading most of your thesis will also remind you of what it contains, and what results and conclusions are reported in it. This is exactly what you need to have in mind when you write or finalize the last chapter in your thesis, the introduction.

Allocate Enough Time for Proofreading

In principle, the chapter order, chapter and section titles and overall structure of your thesis is finalized before you start proofreading. Proofreading is highly important. Experienced examiners describe sloppiness, such as typos and mistakes in referencing, as 'descriptors of a poor thesis'. When stumbling upon such trivial mistakes, it may lead the examiners to think that methods and results—the *research*—aren't rigorous and cannot be trusted (Mullins & Kiley, 2010, p. 378). As a consequence, proofreading is a mandatory part of getting your PhD thesis done and should not be confused with reading most of your thesis to ensure coherence, as described in the previous section. Proofreading is about each and every sentence of your thesis. If, during proofreading, you find that you need to restructure part of your thesis, then do so. Afterwards, start the proofreading over for that part of the thesis, as bigger changes in a document tend to introduce typos and other small mistakes.

Make sure to allocate enough time for careful proofreading. I spent three full days for my own thesis before submission. It would be a shame to spend a few months writing a thesis and then not have a few days for the final polishing. Most of your time and energy should go into proofreading the bulk of your thesis as well as the initial parts of the thesis (cover page, abstract, preface, etc.). But make time to go through appendices and the reference list; more readers than you think are going to look at your reference list, so it, too, needs to be flawless.

Final Words

The thesis is the climax of your PhD project. As for any big undertaking, you should break it into smaller and more manageable bits that you then, one after the other, address and solve. *Plan* your thesis writing and end up with a draft for your table of contents. *Get started* writing, which relies on being able to build up writing momentum. Finally, *get done*, and make your text coherent and tidy. By following this overall philosophy, you may deduce additional tricks and procedures for your specific project and situation (Dunleavy, 2003).

The overall aim is that you turn your thesis writing into 'something that works *for* you, not against you' (Nygaard, 2008, p. 10). By structuring the writing process properly and being conscious about the objective of each of the writing phases, writing the PhD thesis can be a fun and enjoyable process—a process that you may look back on fondly.

References

Dunleavy, P. (2003). *Authoring a PhD: How to plan, draft, write and finish a doctoral thesis or dissertation.* New York, NY: Palgrave Macmillan.

King, S. (2000). *On writing: A memoir of the craft.* New York, NY: Charles Scribner's Sons.

Koenig, K. L., & Schultz, C. H. (2010). *Koenig and Schultz's disaster medicine: Comprehensive principles and practices.* New York, NY: Cambridge University Press.

L'Engle, M. (1984). *The summer of the great-grandmother.* New York, NY: HarperOne.

Mullins, G., & Kiley, M. (2010). 'It's a PhD, not a Nobel Prize': How experienced examiners assess research theses. *Studies in Higher Education, 27*(4), 369–386.

Nygaard, L. P. (2008). *Writing for scholars: A practical guide to making sense and being heard.* Copenhagen: Copenhagen Business School Press.

Pettis, B., & Stark, K. (2017, February 5). *The cult of done manifesto.* Retrieved from http://www.manifestoproject.it/bre-pettis-and-kio-stark/

Single, P. B. (2009). *Demystifying dissertation writing: A streamlined process from choice of topic to final text.* Sterling, VA: Stylus Publishing.

PART TWO

New Opportunities

CHAPTER SIX

I Feel Like a Complete Idiot!

Starting a PhD Program in a New Field

CHRISTINE COX ERIKSSON

Introduction

Many PhD candidates study a subject that they already know quite a bit about, perhaps even after earning a master's degree, working or teaching in the field, or participating in a particular project. However, in some cases, a candidate is chosen for a specific position because they are deemed to possess certain qualities rather than extensive experience in a proposed field of study. I was that type of candidate and soon faced the challenge of being a novice in a field which was new for me.

In 2009, I became one of two doctoral students in a rather ambitious research project on children's early language development and was to receive my degree in the field of Special Education. Most of my previous work experience had involved teaching languages to children as well as adults in a number of contexts. Of course, I was flattered and pleased to be chosen for the PhD project, but I did not anticipate that my journey would be such an emotional rollercoaster. How is it possible for an intelligent, well-educated person to feel like a complete idiot?

This chapter will highlight ways in which it is possible to overcome this feeling through gaining an understanding of the project, and of the field itself. Obviously, the colleagues who brought me onboard felt I was up to the challenge, but it would have been helpful to be reminded that developing the understanding I needed was going to take time. As a doctoral student in a new field you have to acknowledge that orientating yourself in a new discipline is a process that does not happen overnight.

Understanding the Project

Often, a prospective doctoral student will present their own project plan when applying for a position at a Nordic university. At times, it is possible to step into a project that has already been planned by others. A key component in acquiring understanding of a research project that you did not plan yourself is to approach the task with a large dose of enthusiasm and curiosity. It is also useful to know that studying for a PhD in general means progressing through different levels of confusion. In my case, the first level was definitely total confusion!

Entering an Existing Project

If you are thrown into an existing study, spend time carefully reading the funding application for the project. This will provide very useful information regarding the research background, proposed methods, specific research questions, the proposed participants, the time frame, and the instruments for data collection. Read key studies referred to in the research background and prepare questions about them for your project colleagues. It is important to understand what is already known and how your contribution will add to knowledge of the problem area. Ask particular questions about the project design, such as, what will your role be in implementing this project? What do the proposed methods entail? What are the key variables that you will need to understand? You should not hesitate to pester your supervisor and project colleagues with a barrage of questions. After all, they chose you to become part of the project, and your understanding is key to the ultimate success of the project at hand. Write everything down in order to make it more concrete for yourself.

If the research methods are new to you, read articles on other studies which implement these methods. Buy a good general methods textbook, such as Bryman (2008) for social science research, or more specifically, Cohen, Manion, and Morrison (2011) for the field of education. If you are not sure what might be appropriate for your specific field, your supervisor will certainly suggest a suitable methods book. You may have to take some sort of methods course as part of your required course load, and it is a good idea to make sure that you do this early on in your studies. There may even be a specific methods course related to your project that may help you more fully understand the project design.

Application for Ethical Vetting

It is essential to make sure you understand who the project participants are. Research projects involving human participants are always required to make an application to a regional ethical review board. If this has already been done in the existing project, the application is another document you must read and understand. In Sweden, such an application includes a summary of the project, as well as a list of the primary scientific questions which form the basis for the project design. It also contains an overview of the methods which will be used and the nature of the data which will be collected. This will help you understand how the data will help you answer the proposed research questions. The application for ethical vetting will state how records are kept, how the data will be processed, as well as how the participants will be chosen. Ethical aspects are addressed, including issues of informed consent, which details how participants will receive information regarding the project and how consent to their involvement will be obtained.

If the application for ethical vetting has not already been made, being involved in this process will be an excellent way to understand the project and your participation in it. In Sweden, this application must be submitted in Swedish. However, the website (www.epn.se) does give guidance in English on what is required in the application and what sort of information should be provided to the participants.

A New Field of Study

Becoming a PhD student in a new field will certainly involve keeping a great deal of new terms straight in your head. These may be terms regarding research methods, or words such as *empiricism* or *empirical data*. I also remember being confused about words such as *epistemology*, *epidemiology* and *etiology*. When learning about the instrument we used for data collection (see below) I had to constantly remind myself of key terms such as *validity* and *reliability*, and what these meant within the context of our project. Make sure you create a glossary early on where you write detailed notes of terms and explain them in your own words. Keep this up throughout your studies and use the glossary to ask questions regarding terms that you have difficulty explaining yourself.

Instrument

If your project involves collecting data using a specific instrument, you will need to understand this instrument thoroughly. How was it developed and by whom? In our project, we collected some of our data using a parental questionnaire called

Swedish Early Communicative Development Inventories (SECDI) (Berglund & Eriksson, 2000; Eriksson & Berglund, 1999). Reading how SECDI was adapted for the Swedish context from the original American inventory (Fenson et al., 1993, 1994), as well as earlier studies on its development, was extremely helpful. Through this I came to understand how different studies have contributed to the reliability and validity of the instrument we used. I also learned that you should not be afraid to approach the experts on such instruments, or to e-mail authors of the articles you read. Most researchers are happy to find that students in other countries are reading their articles and quite often answer e-mail questions promptly. I even received documents that I had expressed an interest in obtaining.

Analysis Tools

Regardless of whether the data you generate is quantitative or qualitative, you will have to learn about tools for data analysis. Find out what will be required of you and note what is often used in the field in those background articles you read. The vocabulary data we collected was mostly quantitative in nature, requiring that I learn about specific analysis tools, including statistical analysis. If you will be dealing with a large dataset, it will be worth your while to become thoroughly acquainted with a program such as Statistical Package for the Social Sciences (SPSS) or Statistical Analysis System (SAS). It may be wise to take a course or two on SPSS before taking more advanced courses in statistics. Find out whether there are other tools in your field which are readily available through some sort of shared database. I was introduced to the *Child Language Data Exchange System* (CHILDES) database (MacWhinney, 2000), a valuable resource consisting of recordings and transcribed data contributed by child language researchers from around the world. I learned to use the CHAT format (Codes for the Human Analysis of Transcripts) for transcribing our recordings of parent-child interaction, as well as the CLAN programs (Computerized Language Analysis) for analyzing them. Whatever the tool that you need to use, ask your supervisor or other experts for help. Do not hesitate to contacts experts outside of your department or university. It may surprise you how helpful they can be.

Understanding the Field

Another way I reduced my confusion level was to further my understanding of the new field. If your new area is interdisciplinary, try to understand the different strands of research that contribute to the field. Child language research, for example, is conducted by specialists in disciplines such as linguistics, neuroscience and psychology, in addition to special education. When you read the background literature also notice the different journals the articles are published in. This will be a good introduction to the journals you need to follow, especially if you plan to publish.

Publishing

In some fields, it is common to publish articles during the course of your studies. If this is your plan, you may need to understand which journals are relevant to your field of study. You may develop a strategic plan to publish with your supervisor or project colleagues, especially if this is the norm in your specific field. Discuss with your supervisor where and how to strategically publish at a very early stage. The publication process is an area which can be associated with an emotional roller-coaster. It is never a pleasant feeling to receive a rejection letter from a journal, but it is part of academic life. If you do find that you risk not finishing your studies during the allotted time, try to transform your article drafts into a monograph and publish a book instead. In Sweden dissertations are published as books and can be searched for in academic databases.

Conferences in the Field

Learning about a new discipline also means attending key conferences. Find out what these conferences are and attend them with your supervisor or fellow PhD students. I found conferences to be one of the most valuable ways of developing my understanding of who is in the field, as well as what current issues are being discussed. Conferences also give you an appreciation of the history of your field. At a conference in Amsterdam, all attendees were given a special issue of the *Journal of Child Language* which included reflections by leading scholars on advances in research during the first 40 years of the journal. By this time in my studies, I could recognize many of the contributors to this volume, having either read their work, listened to them speak or even met them. You will often find that 'famous name' researchers can be very approachable and down to earth, despite their impressive *Curriculum Vitae.* Don't be afraid of chatting with one of these researchers, should the opportunity arise. It can be helpful to remember that each of these leading researchers was once a novice in the field themselves. See Chapter 8 for more on conferences and getting the most out of them.

Research Networks

Joining national and international research networks can further extend your knowledge. One way to find out about research networks is through signing up for an e-mail list within your field. Do an internet search to see what comes up. Ask your supervisors, project colleagues and fellow PhD students. I was part of a network call *NorPhLex* (Phonological and lexical acquisition in mono- and bilingual children in the Nordic and the Baltic States), which organized seminars and courses for PhD students and other researchers. Since not all universities offer courses in methods of child language research or theories of language acquisition, it was a wonderful opportunity to attend such courses in Sweden and Denmark, as well as other meetings in Norway. Such meetings provide ample opportunities for fruitful networking in both professional and social situations, which lead to an overall increased understanding of your field.

Study Visits

Either in conjunction with an international conference or as a journey on its own, study visits are another valuable way to increase your understanding of a new field. If there is a specific university or research centre that has made significant contributions to your field, make a plan to visit such a site. Start by looking at the centre's website to read about its history and about some of the ongoing research projects. Take the initiative and write an e-mail introducing yourself and your interest in making a study visit to learn about the centre. The person you contact will most certainly forward your mail to someone else if they are not able to accommodate your request themselves.

When I was planning to attend a conference in Canada, I decided to visit an influential research centre in Kansas on the same trip. My gracious host asked what my main objectives for the visit were, and arranged meetings with some of the researchers who had provided inspiration for our project, as well as students and investigators in ongoing research projects. I was also given the opportunity to present our own project in Sweden, which the American researchers found interesting. Visiting the project centre in Kansas City was almost like attending a conference. The walls were covered with large posters that had previously been presented at various venues and I was introduced to a great number of people in the office. I was given a number of articles and brochures explaining their work in special education, which really helped me understand the American context. This was extremely beneficial, given that I had neither studied nor worked in this field before. I attended project meetings and accompanied a therapist on a home visit. The whole experience in turn helped me to understand the research I was reading, as well as to appropriately situate my own research findings within the field later on.

A few years later, I embarked on an additional study visit with my supervisor and another colleague to a large research centre in Wisconsin, which (like the centre in Kansas), was interdisciplinary in nature. Once again, we were graciously received by our hosts who arranged a schedule of meetings, with researchers who gave us insight into the diverse projects at this university centre. I had initiated contact with a Professor whose research I had been reading and was encouraged by her friendly response to ask whether she would make a formal invitation for us to visit. This was needed for us to receive funding for the trip through a special grant for collaboration between educational institutions. Besides further advancing my understanding of the field, the study visit ultimately led to our host becoming my thesis defense opponent a year later.

Conclusion

I finally defended my thesis, slightly more than five years after launching my studies in a new field. Despite occasional feelings of inadequacy, I managed to maintain my enthusiasm and muster all the resourcefulness I could to both survive and succeed. I had to take the initiative to understand my project and the field through reading, learning the necessary tools of the trade, attending conferences and network meetings, and arranging study visits. I certainly do not know everything there is to know, but I no longer feel like an idiot. To quote the supervisor of a fellow doctoral student, 'You will be done when you realize how little you know'.

References

Berglund, E., & Eriksson, M. (2000). Communicative development in Swedish children 16–28 months old: The Swedish early communicative development Inventory—Words and sentences. *Scandinavian Journal of Psychology, 41*(2), 133–144.

Bryman, A. (2008). *Social research methods.* New York, NY: Oxford University Press.

Cohen, L., Manion, L., & Morrison, K. (2011). *Research methods in education* (7th ed.). London: Routledge.

Eriksson, M., & Berglund, E. (1999). Swedish early communicative development inventories: Words and gestures. *First Language, 19*, 55–90.

Fenson, L., Dale, P. S., Reznick, J. S., Bates, E., Thal, D. J., & Pethick, S. J. (1994). Variability in early communicative development. *Monographs of the Society for Research in Child Development, 59*, 1–85.

Fenson, L., Dale, P. S., Reznick, J. S., Thal, D. J., Bates, E., Hartung, J. P., … Reilly, J. S. (1993). *The MacArthur communicative development inventories: User's guide and technical manual.* San Diego, CA: Singular Publishing Group.

MacWhinney, B. (2000). *The CHILDES project: Tools for analyzing talk* (3rd ed.). London: Lawrence Erlbaum.

CHAPTER SEVEN

Returning to Academia

ANNE VORRE HANSEN

Introduction

I never thought of myself as a potential PhD candidate, but, in June 2013, I attended a conference with an Assistant Professor from a Danish University and on the last day of the conference, she encouraged me to apply for an advertised PhD proposal, concerning user-driven innovation in the non-profit sector. So, I gave it a shot, and a week later I was offered a PhD candidacy. The transition from being a project leader at a research institute to beginning as a PhD candidate took place in a very short time. And since I did not know exactly what was expected of me, I began to reflect quite intensively upon what the difference was between practice and academia.

Some of my concerns were related to academic craftsmanship, e.g. when is something actually research and not simply application-oriented studies? Others had to do with project management of the PhD process, and how the PhD candidate can balance being a student and an employee at a university. This chapter focuses on the process of becoming a PhD candidate after years as a practitioner. It specifically highlights the role of the PhD candidate and the main virtues of doing research: thinking and writing. It discusses how increased reflexivity can refine your research and how differences in age and experience can contribute to a rewarding experience amongst PhD candidates. If managed properly, the PhD period can end up being a really joyful time.

The recommendations of this chapter are centered on project management, engaging in rewarding relationships and embracing reflexivity as a condition and an analytical skill to be refined. It pinpoints how the ability to write articles, to keep a focus and realize a goal, (which may be several years ahead), are competencies you, as a PhD candidate, can draw upon in your work life.

The Double Role: Project Manager and PhD Candidate

As a PhD candidate, it is important to appreciate that you are engaged in a dual role—you are both a student and a sort of employee. As an employee, you have a lot of obligations that you are expected to fulfill, and as a student you are learning the skills of academic research. As a result, I prefer the term PhD *candidate* or *fellow* to PhD *student*, since the wording has different connotations and weighting. The following sections elaborate on the task of project management in the PhD project and I will discuss the role as candidate in regard to relationships in the academic world.

The Project Manager

Project management is a crucial part of the PhD process. Although my PhD project to some degree was defined beforehand, I quickly realized that I had been given three years with free rein to manage and define my work life. Although it is enjoyable to sit for days reading philosophy in the sun, you have to approach the PhD time as a project employment. You are expected to deliver a range of quite specific products, such as articles and/or a thesis and you are obliged to realize a number of tasks within a known timeframe. There is no mystery or hidden agenda in this sense.

What might seem difficult is that you have to structure your work yourself—but fortunately there are a lot of project management tools to help you. Use them! Make a plan, make a Work Breakdown Structure (Larsen & Gray, 2011) or make the longest 'to do' list ever. Breaking a huge project down into smaller pieces makes your project manageable and it gives you the pleasure of celebrating your work deadlines along the way. In management lingo, the 'project triangle' (Mac & Madsen, 2013), is a reminder that there is a clear link between time, resources and quality. Research on creativity underscores how structure and frames are foundational for creative thinking (Hennessey & Amabile, 2010). If thinking in terms of project management is new to you, consider it a very important skill to develop.

The Candidate

The academic world is highly hierarchical, and it took me some time to understand that it is not solely dependent on organizational position. Despite age and practical experience, you may, in the beginning, be addressed as a junior colleague. This was not a problem *per se* to me, I was merely puzzled that there was little interest in my network outside academia and in my deep practical knowledge on how to facilitate and engage users in innovation processes. Now that I know the system better I can see that it is also related to an organizational structure based on silos, where a connection and exchange between organizational units working within the same subject field cannot be taken for granted.

As a PhD candidate, find allies that can support your work. The way feedback is given in the academic world can be mystifying (for more on using feedback to further your work, see Chapter 3). I initially experienced feedback from other researchers to be quite disrespectful and non-encouraging. This might have to do with the circumstance that, traditionally in academia, there is an on-going fight for economic resources and prestige. In that sense academia can be characterized by a fault detection culture, which can paradoxically lead to insecurity when you are in a learning position. One of the best pieces of advice I was given from a senior researcher in the beginning of my PhD period was to informally choose some people from my network to be my sort of 'co-supervisors'. I have had approximately five to six colleagues whom I have used to test my arguments and refine my thoughts These are people with whom I think better, get ideas from and laugh with. Some are researchers themselves (at varying level of experience) whereas others are practitioners.

Share your ideas and thoughts with these allies and other PhD candidates. This can lead to rewarding relationships—especially if you dare to be honest concerning the things that you experience as difficult. I have learned a lot from my younger colleagues since they had an updated theoretical overview and knowledge on the organizational structures at the university that I could draw upon. In return, I believe that I contributed with the experience and confidence to say out loud what some of the younger candidates only dared thinking. Sharing experiences and challenges is a way to normalize your own private concerns, and lead to further learning.

Across age, experience, and professions there are people who make your mind expand and some that make your ideas diminish. You need both, at different times—but mostly you need to engage in relations with the former. I am a social person and a team player, so the entrance to my PhD was hard in regard to lack of collaboration and knowledge sharing, as there was not a lively work environment at my institution. When I realized that most researchers actually do want to engage in a good respectful discussion of science and theory, I became happy to work in an environment with very skilled and analytically sharp people.

The Virtues of Research: Thinking and Writing

My return to academia involved an introduction to both analytical processes and work practices, namely, the activities of thinking and writing.

The Process of Thinking

After half a year as a PhD candidate I had to ask a former colleague, who at that time had become an Associate Professor, how the work I was doing as a PhD candidate was different from what we had been doing as a consultant. The background for the question was my own insecurity about whether I was in fact doing research, since the tools and methods I applied were basically the same as in my consultancy business (surveys, in-depth interviews, observations and workshops). I have always been an investigative practitioner. Nevertheless, the immediate answer to my question was—the level of *reflexivity*.

Reflexivity is considered an ethical responsibility because reflection asks us to look at ourselves and consider what type of person, or what type of researcher we have been and aspire to be. Reflexivity is a scientific virtue (Alvesson, Hardy, & Harley, 2008) and an essential part of what theory/theorizing is. Reflexivity is related to *what* kind of knowledge we produce as researchers and also *how* we generate new insights. In this sense, we need to consider the quality of the questions we raise as researchers and how they are positioned within a theoretical framework. Practitioners solve concrete challenges, whereas researchers, by discussing theory and empirical data to understand what is at stake, contribute with questions that refine practice (at least within management) by pinpointing some concerns that might reveal new thinking and practices.

The Process of Writing

'Write from day one' is standard advice to new PhD candidates. I was a bit worried about this since I had not realized that being a researcher is mainly about writing and dissemination. I did not perceive myself to be a writer; before beginning the PhD project I was solely writing power-point reports as a consultant. The thought of writing more than 100 pages seemed quite scary. However, my thoughts on what a text is and what writing processes are has changed. I came to realize that I was continuously producing quite a lot of text. I took notes at presentations, I kept a logbook with unfinished thoughts, notes from formal and informal meetings, ideas and quotes, and I had written short text pieces as part of my subscriptions to PhD courses. Those writings became a fruitful basket of work that I dived into when I began writing my publications and the thesis itself.

An important aspect of writing is that you can write a bit ahead of your analysis—you may not have realized the full range of your argument before beginning to write. Go with your hunch and trust the analysis to become clearer along the way since writing and analysis is an intertwined iterative process. The writing process as a PhD candidate, where you write, then re-write and then write again, might seem frustrating, but in the end your text gets better, which makes the effort worth it.

Conclusion

In addition to becoming a kind of 'certified' researcher due to the PhD title you obtain skills during the process, which are both distinct and useful. These skills include project management, the ability to assess a huge amount of data and/or text and pinpoint the most relevant issues, heightened awareness and an intensified analytical sense, and writing skills. In addition, you also develop a high degree of confidence and credibility.

The PhD process can be both lonely and hard, especially if you are returning to academia. It is time to come up with a new narrative: the PhD process is probably the only time in your life where you can do some thorough thinking and reflection for a sustained period of time. When you have been working as a practitioner, this level of experience is a gift, and I hope that candidates who come directly from academia will embrace this too.

References

Alvesson, M., Hardy, C., & Harley, B. (2008). Reflecting on reflexivity: Reflexive textual practices in organization and management theory. *Journal of Management Studies, 45*(3), 480–501.

Hennessey, B. A., & Amabile, T. M. (2010). Creativity. *Annual Review of Psychology, 61*, 569–598.

Larsen, E., & Gray, C. (2011). *Project management: The managerial process.* New York, NY: McGraw-Hill Irwin.

Mac, A., & Madsen, S. (2013). Metoder til rationel styring af projekter. In A. Mac & P. Hagedorn-Rasmussen (Eds.), *Projektarbejdets kompleksitet: viden, værktøjer og læring* (pp. 183–100). Frederiksberg: Samfundslitteratur.

CHAPTER EIGHT

But Do I Really Have Anything to Say?

Conferences and the PhD Student

BETHANNE PAULSRUD

Introduction

At first, you are just happy to become a doctoral student at a Nordic university. You refine your research plan, you meet your supervisors, you take your courses, and maybe you even start field or lab work. You create a community with your fellow students. Then the conference announcements start trickling in: you see a call for papers in the copy room or you sign up for an e-mail list and receive notices of exciting gatherings around the world.

Attending conferences is not only for the accomplished and seasoned researcher. Attending conferences is for all researchers at any stage of their career. A goal of any conference is, 'to bring together scholars for the purpose of sharing *ongoing* research' (Semenza, 2005, p. 181). I submitted a contribution to my first conference less than six months after commencing my program of PhD studies. Did I have results? No, but I had a research plan and had started some pilot work. This is what I presented at the conference, and the feedback I received from senior researchers with vast expertise in my area was invaluable. This first experience made me realize the importance of conference participation and the integral role it plays in your PhD studies—even before your results are complete. By the time I earned my doctorate, I had attended 15 conferences, presenting my ongoing research to a large number of people. What did I learn from all this conferencing? A lot.

There are many advantages to sending that abstract off—and even more advantages to actually attending national and international conferences. This chapter walks you through some key points about conference attendance, focusing on the steps you need to take before, during and after the conference. Soon, you will be busy searching for conferences.

Before the Conference

Finding the Right One

Your first step in reaching the wonderful world of conferences is to actually *find* the conferences in your field. This is done in several ways, besides scanning the bulletin boards in the copy room or corridors at your department. One way is to subscribe to online lists that cater to different fields. Receiving daily or weekly digests of subject-specific lists will keep you informed not only of new books and theses in your area of research, but also of future conferences. If you are not sure where to find these lists, ask around. Your PhD colleagues with more experience, as well as your supervisors, will surely have some tips. You can also search the Internet for recurring conferences in your field, as this can lead you to upcoming events. The websites for these often have mailing lists to keep potential attendees in the loop.

Preparing an Abstract

To apply for active participation at a conference, you need to write an abstract. Follow the guidelines carefully as far as word count, formatting, and information requested. Some conference organizers want an author bio note; others do not. Some may require references, while others do not. If the call for papers is unclear or lacks specifications about such details, contact the organisers directly for clarification. Also, find the program from previous conferences by the same research association or network to see how previous presenters have written their abstracts to get an idea of the style.

Writing the abstract is valuable practice in communicating your research concisely to an unknown audience—one great advantage of aiming for conference participation. Describing your research succinctly is an important skill, one that requires practice and honing. The reviewers are not your supervisors who know your work intimately. Rather, they are peers from the community who may only have a limited prior knowledge of your specific topic but who need to understand what you are doing just by reading your abstract. Their feedback helps you to get an idea of how your work is going. Hickson writes:

> The submission of papers to a conference provides a relatively quick evaluation of your work. Whereas sending a paper to a journal can take months or years, the turn-around time for paper evaluations is considerably less. Very often, competitive paper presentations provide authors with a set of independent evaluations from their peers. Acceptance of a competitively selected conference paper is the first step in eventually getting a paper published. With a critic or respondent to your paper on the panel, you have completed step 2. Here, an 'expert' provides you with first-hand, direct advice about how to move forward with your scholarship. (2006, p. 466)

However, sometimes you do not know exactly what your results will be by the time of the conference. If you are in the middle of an ongoing study, write that. It is perfectly fine to be honest and say that you are presenting an ongoing study and to describe your preliminary results at the time of the abstract. Again, read through those previous abstracts to get an idea of how researchers suggest presentations of work-in-progress. Do not forget that your short text will be published in the conference program and is intended to entice participants to come and listen to you. Be clear and concise, but also creative and catchy, especially in the title of the abstract. When browsing through the conference program, most people only skim titles, so choose yours carefully. Revise your abstract several times, and then ask another PhD student or your supervisor to read it for feedback. Before you send it off, double and triple check spelling and grammar.

Knowing you will present at a conference in the near future makes you get things done, which is another advantage of writing an abstract and anticipating the presentation. Applying for a conference creates a deadline for yourself and your work—perhaps one of the few hard deadlines you have during your PhD project. If you, for example, in your abstract indicate that your analysis of a certain number of interviews or your collection of a certain number of samples will be presented, you have a very concrete incentive to get that done.

Preparing you Presentation

While the exact format can differ—*always* check the guidelines provided by the organizers—a typical conference presentation is about 15–25 minutes for presenting, and 5–10 minutes for questions and discussion. At many conferences, the norm is to use PowerPoint slides for the presentation. Think carefully about how many slides you need to present your work and deliver a message about your research. I often hear about one slide per minute as a rule of thumb, but think more about what you need to say and how you can say it in the time allotted than the number of slides. Chose a font size that is legible and keep text on the slides to a minimum—you do not want your audience to read a long text instead of listening to you. Practice the entire presentation several times before you even leave for the conference, and revise to improve its flow. Many presentations can be 'dry and, well, *academic*' (Semenza, 2005, p. 191), so do what you can to avoid being a boring, unprepared presenter.

During the Conference

Make a Plan

The daily program is usually available online prior to the conference. Read it and make a plan for the sessions or talks you would like to attend. Print it or save it on your computer. Better yet, check if there is a conference app you can download to plan your conference days. Be strategic: Are there certain 'hotshots' in your field you do not want to miss? Is there a researcher you may like to collaborate with in the future? Try to meet that person before or after their presentation and suggest a cup of coffee together. At the same time, do not plan a schedule with wall-to-wall sessions that will not leave you time and energy to digest the talks and input you get. Decide the most important slots you cannot miss and also schedule some breathing room for yourself to chat randomly with others, review your own notes, or to simply rest a bit. Conferences can be exhausting. Conferences usually start by 8 or 9 in the morning, with sessions until the evening, often followed by official dinners or informal get-togethers with new and old contacts. You may actually get less rest at a conference than you do at home. Make sure to allocate time to browse the publishers' corner, where you will find new journals, textbooks and theoretical volumes in your field (Hickson, 2006). Publishers are people who are important to your academic career, so introduce yourself and make that personal contact (Renck Jalongo & Machado, 2016). They may remember you later when you submit a manuscript.

Be flexible about your planning, as once at the conference, you may realize changes are necessary. Sometimes, a change is required because the conference venue is so large that you simply cannot get from one room to another in good time between two interesting presentations. You may also like to change your plans after making new contacts in your field, as this may lead to your decision to attend their sessions.

Giving Your Presentation

When it is finally time for your presentation, arrive early to the room and test *all* equipment you will use. Dress smart, but do not diverge from your usual style. If you are uncomfortable in your outfit, you will be painfully aware of this and spend your short few minutes tugging at your clothes rather than focusing on your brilliantly prepared talk. At your presentation, start by introducing yourself (Renck Jalongo & Machado, 2016). Look at the audience and not your slides or papers. Breathe, and speak at a natural pace. Be organised and help your audience to know what is coming up, for example, a simple statement like, 'Next, I will present my results' (Semenza, 2005). If a microphone is provided, use it. In some branches of research, it is common to offer a small handout (perhaps A5 size) with your abstract and your contact details. This is better than offering copies of your entire presentation for two reasons: you may not want to widely distribute your ongoing work, and it is less paper for people to take.

It may happen that, despite the best intentions and self-assigned deadlines, you are not ready with the results you promised in your abstract all those months ago. For example, those applying for the World Congress of Applied Linguistics (AILA) must submit an abstract more than a year in advance and a lot can change in a research project in this period. Presenting on-going work and preliminary conclusions is quite normal at conferences. It is also acceptable to present an analysis of your own methodology as part of your work in-progress. That is, how have your methods been working for you? Do you have reflections on your methodological choices or experiences that may be helpful to another researcher? Perhaps you have developed a new method based on a common one in your field. The obstacles and victories along the way in your research can be as interesting and revealing to fellow researchers as the few results you have, so talk about this. Think of your presentation and participation as a document of your progress and work (Renck Jalongo & Machado, 2016).

Audience Feedback

After presenting your work, the audience may provide valuable feedback to help you continue your research. Questions may help you to refine your study or to consider your preliminary results in a new light. Consider either audio-recording the discussion at your presentation, such as using your phone, or asking a colleague to write down questions and suggestions from audience members (you can later return the favour). Be open to dialogue and not defensive about critical questions. If you do not understand a question, ask for clarification. You participate as a PhD student and are there to learn in addition to contributing, and it is perfectly fine to say you do not know about a certain theory or method that someone from the audience may suggest as a better alternative. Be gracious, acknowledge the contribution, and suggest that you continue the conversation over coffee following the presentation. After all, networking is another crucial component of conference participation.

Networking

The value of networking cannot be overestimated. You will meet both top researchers in your field as well as fellow PhD students from outside of your home university—all people who may play important roles in your future academic career. I met my future defence opponent at a conference, and establishing contact with her paved the way to her participation in my examination. Chat with the people sitting near you at the presentations. Ask them why they chose that session or what their own research is about. Bring business cards and exchange them with those you meet. Aim to meet a variety of people from diverse contexts. It may be tempting for Nordic students to stick together for safety and comfort, but try to push yourself to talk with others rather than just your own colleagues. If you stay at the conference hotel, sit down at breakfast with others also wearing name tags and ask them what they are presenting. Plan to attend most of the offered social activities, such as the conference dinner or opening reception. Mingle and do not be shy about introducing yourself to others. While you may experience an 'intimidation factor' when meeting your academic gurus (Hickson, 2006, p. 464), remember that 'doctoral students hold the primary responsibility of forming bridges with their peers *and* significant scholars' (Ghosh & Githens, 2009, p. 3). See the conference as a way of advertising you and your work. You want people to remember your name (Semenza, 2005).

After the Conference

Follow Up

Once you get home, follow up with the new contacts you met and chatted with. The conference is a way to 'become part of a network of lifelong professional and personal friends' (Hickson, 2006, p. 465). Simply send an e-mail and write that you enjoyed meeting them and hope to keep in touch. If you talked about a specific topic, send an article or link that the other person may be interested in. After meeting a German PhD student at one conference I sent her announcements of upcoming conferences in our field, and she reciprocated with similar tips. We also kept each other updated on the progress in our work, which was an additional source of inspiration. If you enjoyed a certain presentation, contact the researcher to request the presentation or the references, even if you did not speak with that person yourself. Presenters are always pleased to know that people enjoyed the talk enough to follow up. If you use social media for work, such as Twitter or a professional blog, consider sharing a link with your new researcher colleagues.

If your new contacts are in your city, arrange visits or seminars to your department. Check with your department if there is funding to finance such a visit, as visiting researchers who present a seminar or workshop are usually welcome. After I met a prominent Japanese professor at several conferences, we jointly arranged a research visit to my university. His lecture was well-attended, he made new contacts, and we had the chance to catch up on recent news in our field.

Publishing Opportunities

Some conferences offer to publish in edited volumes, which may provide you with a much-needed publication if you are writing a thesis by compilation or just need a venue for your first results. Have this in mind before you attend the conference. If your presentation has the possibility to be reworked into an article or chapter, start writing this even before the conference. Not only will this help you with your presentation, but it may help you manage the deadlines for the subsequent volume, as they can be tight. One conference I attended sent a call for full papers with a deadline of only one month.

Your proposal was peer-reviewed for the conference, so your abstract has already been given the stamp of approval by experts in the field. Think of your carefully written and revised abstract as a 'helpful starting point for a journal article or book chapter'. If your presentation was 'well-attended and well-received', you can feel confident 'that peers found it interesting and that it effectively conveyed the purpose' (Renck Jalongo & Machado, 2016, p. 118). If you aim for publication in the conference proceedings, follow the guidelines and deadlines carefully, just as you did with the abstract.

Review and Plan Ahead

Review and summarize your conference notes once you are back home. You may find that you have new references to read, new methods to try out, and new perspectives to consider. I usually kept all of my conference notes in one place and regularly reviewed them throughout the research and writing process of my dissertation. I found that I often discovered things later that were not as applicable at the time, but when I read the notes again, they suddenly became very relevant. Reviewing your notes and browsing through the conference program can also help you to plan ahead. You may decide to submit an abstract to the next conference arranged by that particular network. You may also decide to keep an eye out for certain speakers at upcoming conferences. At the conferences you attend, you may learn about special interest groups or research networks in your field, and joining these will help you learn about upcoming conferences (Hickson, 2006).

Share

Schedule time to share your conference experience with your colleagues. If you did not give your presentation in your department prior to the conference, offer to do so in a seminar afterwards. Let your colleagues know about the feedback you got and how this may affect your continued work. Either formally, such as at a staff meeting, or informally, such as in the lunchroom or on coffee break, share your own highlights from the conference. Describe the best speakers, new methods or new resources. Bring the programme for others to see, and share your conference review and summary with them. You may also like to summarize the most interesting talks and topics from the conference in writing and share that small overview with your colleagues.

Conclusion

Conference participation is not just a form of academic tourism, but full of advantages and a key component of the life of any Nordic PhD student. Some universities even require participation in a national or international conference at some point during your PhD studies. Through conference attendance and participation, you gain experience from writing the abstract and presenting work-in-progress, you get inspiration from listening to others, you widen your network, and you get possibilities for publishing—all invaluable experiences to both your studies and your future career as an academic. Hickson compares it to a 'professional equivalent of the Thanksgiving Dinner. Several generations of the "family" come together year after year and share meals, news, successes, and failures' (Hickson, 2006, p. 467). Think of a conference as a family dinner: you meet those you find it difficult to talk with as well as those you are very excited to see. This chapter has guided you through the three aspects of conference attendance: Before, during and after the conference. Now that you know about all the possibilities and advantages, it is time to go find a conference.

References

Ghosh, R., & Githens, R. P. (2009). Application of social network theory: Doctoral students' experiences in conferences. *New Horizons in Adult Education and Human Resource Development, 23*(1), 25–28.

Hickson, M. (2006). Raising the question #4. Why bother attending conferences? *Communication Education, 55*(4), 464–468.

Renck Jalongo, M., & Machado, C. (2016). *Making effective presentations at professional conferences. A guide for teachers, graduate students and professors* (1st ed.). Cham (ZG): Springer International Publishing.

Semenza, G. M. C. (2005). *Graduate study for the twenty-first century: How to build an academic career in the humanities.* New York, NY: Palgrave Macmillan.

PART THREE

Wellbeing and Support

CHAPTER NINE

Maintaining Your Mental Health All the Way Through the PhD Process

KAMMA OVERGAARD HANSEN

> Carrie is standing alone in her living room, staring at the wall. Photographs, maps, tickets, prints, transcribed telephone conversations, handwritten notes … all form a complex, collage-like archive over all the traces in her current case. Carrie is pulling strings from one element to another. Carrie is organizing all the elements in colour. Carrie forgets to eat. Carrie stays up all night. Carrie is going mad.
>
> —CUESTA, GIDEON, GANSA, & GORDON (2011: SEASON 1, EPISODE 1–12)

Introduction

Fans of the TV series *Homeland* will probably recognize this description of its main character, CIA officer Carrie Mathison, who is brave and brilliant—but suffering from bipolar disorder. Carrie takes great risks, crosses borders, and sacrifices practically everything in her struggle to solve a case, while being met with skepticism and disbelief (Cuesta, Gideon, Gansa, & Gordon, 2011–2013: season 1–3). As art historian W. J. T. Mitchell has put it, she is suffering from a 'Cassandra-complex': Being *blessed* with the ability to predict the future but *cursed* in that nobody is ever going to believe her (Mitchell, 2015).

Your PhD process will probably not be quite as terrifying as Carrie's struggle with international terrorism and disbelieving colleagues, yet the PhD process might occasionally be filled with desperation, loneliness, skepticism, and growing madness. Three years of doctoral research is three years stuck with a project where you are the only real expert. No matter how nice your fellow PhD students are, how considerate your supervisor is, and how understanding your family and friends might be, you may eventually feel very alone. Meanwhile, working with complicated theory on a daily basis is a brain marathon in itself.

This chapter will discuss whether negative feelings and mental danger signals can be avoided in the process of writing a PhD—and whether they even *should* be completely avoided. Is mental instability a necessary—and perhaps even fruitful—part of a long, creative academic process? If it is, what is a sufficient amount of insanity?

In this chapter, I will suggest some strategies for maintaining your mental health and encourage a higher degree of self-acceptance through the challenges you will face during the PhD process. It is my intention to pave the way for a more honest approach to minor mental health disorders, which are a potential issue in any academic work environment, and particularly among PhD students. You can read this chapter as an elementary guide to the warning signals that you as a PhD student should not ignore, and as a tool to remain self-analytical and self-caring, all the way through your PhD study.

Taking Care of Your Brain

Presumably, the majority of us precede our PhD studies with high ambitions and a great amount of enthusiasm. You have worked hard to obtain your scholarship and you are excited about the privileged prospect of spending the next three or four years developing your thesis and contributing to the field of research. It *is* exciting! You have already done extremely well just getting there. However, the exhaustion of your brain has already commenced.

Writing your application is a task. Switching between English and your native language is a task. Meeting new people and getting to know new colleagues is a task. Basically, everything that is new to your brain is training, but can also be an extra burden. Surviving and succeeding PhD study challenges your ability to take care of your brain in a very concrete manner. As trivial as it may sound, you need to sleep, eat, and exercise in order to keep your brain (and body) fit for all the challenges you will be putting it through during your PhD study. You need to avoid long periods of Carrie-like, manic intellectual activity.

Sleep

First of all, you need sleep. Professor Henning Kirk, a renowned Danish researcher in the field of ageing, has described the remarkable benefits that the brain earns from a good night's sleep. Not only does sleep have a considerable impact on response time and concentration, it also helps you memorize the new information you have collected during the day. The processes that the brain goes through during sleep are literally a 'brain wash', as the brain cleanses its neurons, enabling them to perform necessary chemical processes while the brain is awake and active (Kirk, 2014).

Of course, these benefits depend on the *quality* of your sleep. Keep a regular circadian rhythm; no coffee or big meals late in the evening; no hard-physical activity during the last hours before bedtime; no laptop, cell phone, or paper work in bed; and remember to exercise during the week, as physical activity will induce natural fatigue. If you start falling asleep in front of your desk at daytime, do *not* just drink more coffee as you scorn yourself for being undisciplined and weak. Like many living in the north, you may be suffering from a lack of Vitamin D and a quick blood test will tell you if this is the case. We tend to blame ourselves for being lazy when we lose concentration and have difficulties staying awake when we need to. Instead, we ought to focus on reasons and constructive solutions.

Stress

Think of your brain as a muscle that craves both training and rest. Remember that any kind of mental struggling is a task for your brain—cracking theoretical codes as well as handling all sorts of personal stuff.

Although to most people it might sound alluring to spend three to four years working on your own project, scheduling your own work hours, and concentrating on one of your main interests, there will be times when your employment as a PhD candidate can be extremely hard. People tend to forget that part of the employment as a PhD candidate is not research, but a considerable amount of other responsibilities such as teaching, arranging seminars, editing research publications, and participating in all sorts of meetings. Meanwhile, you need to design the process of your own research and figure out a structure that enables you to keep track of all your ideas, cases, and empirical material. That can be stressful and frightening, and this can lead to a more permanent stress condition, such as depression.

People suffering from depression are often lacking specific neurotransmitters known as noradrenaline and norepinephrine, as are people diagnosed with Attention Deficit Hyperactivity Disorder (ADHD) (Alban, 2016; Bilenberg, 2013). You have every reason to be concerned if you lose concentration for more than a few weeks. Short term stress might enable you to concentrate intensely for a short period of time, but as every other part of your body, your brain will eventually get exhausted and reduce its performance. Feeling that you need to perform at a high level all the time, combined with a decreasing ability to perform at all, is a dangerous cocktail. It is important to catch some of the symptoms before you find yourself with an actual psychiatric diagnosis.

You may be familiar with some of the more common stress symptoms: irritability, loss of memory, loss of concentration, fatigue, lack of appetite, insomnia, headache, stomach pain, and irregular heartbeat, to name a few. Three basic pieces of advice that I personally spent all three years of my PhD study trying to integrate into my daily life are: Do something other than work. It is tempting to let go of hobbies as well as one's social life when you are hung up at work. Preferably, find something that you are good at and that can provide you with tangible and immediate experiences of success. Relax your brain. Do not spend your breaks talking about your PhD project or skimming through your Facebook news feed. Do nothing. Look out the window, meditate, or take a walk. Relieve the pressure on your brain. Stop demanding of yourself to memorize everything. Write memos, sticky notes, and shopping lists; use the calendar function of your phone for appointments; clear off your desk frequently; and take your time figuring out a system for archiving all the stuff that might be useful to you later in your PhD project.

Impostor Syndrome

'Impostor Syndrome' is common among young scientists and can be extremely stressful. Impostor Syndrome covers the constant feeling of not having deserved your success followed by fear of being exposed as a fraud (Clance & Imes, 1978). Take it from someone who has been there, it can actually be quite counterproductive. Having coincidentally learned that my lousy academic self-esteem in fact had a name, I soon experienced that I was not alone. Starting out as idle chat by the coffee machine, one after another of my PhD colleagues admitted the same feelings.

Knowing that everyone around you might be feeling as insecure as yourself is probably not going to help you all that much in the long run, but this is one part where we can actually learn something from our high-risk CIA officer, Carrie Mathison: In order to get on with your research, you must lie and cheat. Only not about your field of research, but to some extent about who you are.

In 2012, social psychologist Amy Cuddy gave a TED talk concerning body language and self-esteem (Cuddy, 2012). In her talk, Cuddy presents how our nonverbal gestures not only *describe* who we are, but also *define* who we are. Grabbing your arms, crossing your legs, and rubbing your neck all make you look smaller—and feel smaller. Likewise, open arms and loose legs let you take up more space, literally as well as figuratively. In her research, Cuddy has proved that so-called 'power poses' make our testosterone level increase as our amount of the stress hormone cortisol decreases. In other words, a powerful body language is extremely useful as a strategic weapon against Impostor Syndrome. Not only can you 'fake it till you make it'; you can actually fake it 'till you become it' (Cuddy, 2012).

The Right Amount of Insanity

You have a lot to win from a healthy life style, a structured day, and suitable body language. However, a small outbreak of insanity from time to time seems to be inevitable in the life of a PhD student. Just like Carrie, you will need to keep yourself locked on target for periods of time and those periods of time may very well be the best parts of life as a PhD student, researcher, or scientist. However, long-term experiences of academic flow will make you temporarily remote and emotionally fragile. Firstly, because you will be working with your own project so intensely that it becomes your whole world for a while, and secondly, because you will simply get exhausted. That is not necessarily a problem, but it requires some care and understanding from people around you. You will *not* be fit for handling complicated family issues or solving a love-life crisis while finishing your dissertation. Quite the contrary, you will need all the rest and self-care you can mobilize at the moment. You can call it temporary insanity, or fragility. Either way, you need to embrace it and forgive yourself for neglecting other parts of your life.

The PhD process is a unique opportunity to develop your thesis, to follow your academic instincts, to test your theoretical ideas in a stimulating academic environment, and to create your very own contribution to your favorite field of research. To your employer, assigning you with the PhD position in the first place is an investment in you as a promising talent who is expected to take science to a new level within your field. Ask anyone who has made it all the way to the top in any field of sports, music, art, or science, and they will probably say the same thing: Success comes with a price. Nobody has ever won the Olympics without several years of hard training and personal struggle behind them. Talents do not evolve without *some* amount of blood, sweat, and tears.

The million-dollar question is, of course, what is the right amount of insanity? When is frustration, distraction, and stress just a temporary condition, and when has it become permanent? In the ideal world, your supervisor is keeping an eye on you, encouraging you when you are about to give up, and ordering you to rest when you are obviously burning out. Succeeding as a PhD candidate is a matter of recognizing when you have reached the maximum of your ability to figure things out by yourself. You might have a lot to win from seeking specified help instead of just borrowing an ear from whoever is available at the moment and willing to agree with you concerning complaint you may have. Seek *qualified* help when you need to.

Seeking Help

If the situation has reached a more serious level, you are obliged to tell your supervisor. Most supervisors will be friendly and helpful once you find yourself crying in their office. Yet it can be constructive if you identify at least the outline of your current struggle by yourself before knocking on your supervisor's door. In my experience, writing can help you do that: Set the timer for 15 minutes, let go of your vanity, write whatever occurs to your mind, and do not stop until the alarm goes off. You can use this method as a preparation for yourself before talking to your supervisor (or whichever help you are seeking) or as a first draft of an e-mail to your supervisor. Seeking help, seeking it the right way and at the right time is a task in itself and the importance of it should not be underestimated.

In *Homeland*, Carrie's sister has the role of forcing Carrie off work when her manic symptoms increase (Gansa & Gordon, 2011–2013). Considering that in your life as a PhD candidate you might be studying abroad and probably seeking isolation for some periods of time, you need to take on that role yourself. One way is to set up some rules for yourself in advance: For exactly *how* many days in a row is insomnia acceptable for you? How many times in a row is it OK to skip exercise? How many incidents of conflict with your closest relatives fall within the span of a normal relationship? What are the palpable symptoms that should bring you to an *immediate* stop? Whether it is palpitations, three days of constant nausea, or sudden outbursts of crying that you define as *your* ultimate symptoms of a high-risk situation, it can be an idea to define them *before* things go wrong. Once you are at the level of a breakdown, you might not be adequately analytical to define what is going on. However, some well-structured, mental preparation can prevent you from some of the emotional extremes.

Conclusion

This chapter has emphasized the importance of self-structuring, meta-reflection, and self-caring as part of your survival package concerning staying well. I have pointed out the importance of sleep; of preventing yourself from stress through immediately rewarding activities, recharging breaks, and structured working routines; of power posing as a way to increase your academic self-esteem; of embracing your momentarily insanity as a natural part of developing your talent; and of seeking qualified help in a planned way. I discussed some of the results from psychological and medical science that may be fruitful to keep in mind when commencing your career as a PhD candidate and possible future scientist. As with any self-help guide, there might be moments when you are impervious to all kinds of reason and good advice. Do not despair. Some amount of tears have to be cried during your PhD process, and considering your sense of reason and knowledge about the brain, you will find your way back on track. After all, as far as we know, even the fictional character of Carrie Mathison survives her terrifying ordeals.

References

Alban, D. (2016). Norepinephrine—A key player in stress, depression, and ADHD. Retrieved from http://reset.me/story/norepinephrine-a-key-player-in-stress-depression-and-adhd/

Bilenberg, N. (2013). Hvad er ADHD? *Netdoktor.* Retrieved from http://www.netdoktor.dk/sygdomme/fakta/damp.htm

Clance, P. R., & Imes, S. A. (1978). The imposter phenomenon in high achieving women: Dynamics and therapeutic intervention. *Psychotherapy: Theory, Research and Practice, 15*(3), 241–247.

Cuddy, A. (2012). *Your body language shapes who you are.* Retrieved from https://www.ted.com/talks/amy_cuddy_your_body_language_shapes_who_you_are#t-1233653

Cuesta, Michael, et al. (Directors), Raff, Gideon (Writer), Gansa, Alex & Gordon, Howard (Developers for American television). (2011–2013). Homeland, season 1–3. In Gansa, A., et al. (Executive producers), *Homeland.* New York City, NY: Showtime Networks, Inc.

Kirk, H. (2014). *Sådan holder du hjernen skarp.* Netdoktor: Retrieved from http://www.netdoktor.dk/sundhed/hjerneiform.html

Mitchell, W. J. T. (2015, September 21). Method, madness, and montage. Key note presentation. *Word and Image*, Aarhus University, Aarhus, Denmark.

CHAPTER TEN

My Disability Does Not Define Me

BETHANY ROGERS

Introduction: Setting the Bar Higher

Whether you are an international student considering a PhD program in the Nordic countries, or you are a Scandinavian considering further study, this chapter is written to help those with a disability (physical or mental, visible or invisible) navigate expectations and important relationships within the university. The advice here is based on my experience as well as those of several friends throughout the Nordic countries.

Everyone's experience with disability is different. Like any struggle in life, it is a heaving torrent of ups and downs. It comes with its own emotional journey, from the choppy waters of misdiagnoses or bad medicine, to deep rivers of frustration and anger. As a PhD student, you will have to learn to navigate these waters like any Viking warrior and make it to Lindisfarne in time for the burning (also known as 'when funding runs out').

As a person with cerebral palsy, it's a habit of mine to minimize my disability whenever possible, to the point where I have occasionally arranged to meet people sitting down so that their first impression of me isn't clouded by the strangeness of my movement (I walk with a pronounced limp). If I could say one thing to many of the well-meaning people I meet who speak to me about my disability, it would be this: I am no one's inspiration because I am disabled. 'Inspiration porn' is when disabled people are called inspirational for doing all the things that able-bodied people do. If you find me inspiring because I am a fierce researcher, a dedicated historian or an all-around boss, by all means, drink in my magnificence.

When I was in the process of earning an MA in Education, I took a year off to teach English in Taiwan. I wanted so badly to prove myself—to prove that I could do the job as well as my able-bodied co-workers. I volunteered for every opportunity to substitute. I did every extra activity, parent evening, and special performance that came my way. Like many first-year teachers, I exhausted myself mentally and emotionally. I wanted to be given a leadership position within the school I was working at, and to have my own kindergarten class. Kindergarten teachers had a more stable schedule and higher pay, and I went after it like a feral wolverine because I wanted it so bad. The head teacher came to me, sat me down and said, 'We have two openings in the kindergarten right now …' My heart leapt, I was so excited; I was achieving my goal!

Then, the teacher took a deep breath and eyed me carefully. '… But I'm not going to give it to you. Some of our parents might not like the way you walk and they may complain.' I worked at a cram school, which hires foreigners without qualification to teach children English after the regular school day is done. I was the only person at my branch that actually had educational training. Everyone on staff agreed that I was excellent at my work and yet I was being denied what I wanted for the way I was born.

I hit my head on that bar I set so high, and I was devastated.

Attitudes toward disability are different around the world, and being rejected so blatantly made me question everything. A study comparing American and Taiwanese college students showed a significant difference in the way disability is perceived. Taiwanese students held some of the most conservative viewpoints: 'In Chinese culture, the perceived stigma of disability is especially strong and frequently associated with the belief in current or past sins of the parents. Lack of knowledge about disability, especially about mental disabilities, contributes to the misperception about the effect of disability on one's offspring' (Chen, Brodwin, Cardoso, & Fong, 2002, p. 10).

Years later, I found myself in Iceland, studying medieval history. In other countries, when meeting people, I would often hear, 'Are you … ok?' with vague gestures at my lower extremities, or 'What's that about?' In Iceland, and in other Nordic travels, I have not had any negative experiences, but I am who my experiences have made me. I remember the twinge of fear I felt when, on meeting the eminent scholar who would become my supervisor; I caught him giving me a curious look as we walked down the hall together. I knew it was the 'What's wrong with you?' look, but he only smiled at me. We've never discussed my disability, as I don't require any accommodations.

I was cheered immensely the first time I read stanza 71 of the Old Norse *Hávamál*: 'The lame man rides a horse, the handless man drives a herd, the deaf man fights and succeeds; to be blind is better than to be burnt; a corpse is of no use to anyone' (Snorri, 2014, p. 23). I could still be useful here. To myself, to my field, to the world. The wound I received in Taiwan began to heal, but the scar is still there, like the others I have. New challenges appeared instead.

At the start of my PhD research, feelings of hopelessness I had powered through (and ignored) for years were suddenly a shrieking chorus of doubt and self-hatred. I was overwhelmed by the simplest tasks. Academic articles, which had before laid the secrets of history at my feet, became incomprehensible vocabulary exercises for my overtaxed concentration. There is a sensation, as you are about to fall, when you don't know if you will catch yourself and go on with your day, or make that painful impact with the ground. I felt that sensation in the pit of my stomach, 24 hours a day.

I have since been diagnosed with generalized anxiety disorder and depression and have worked to find things that really work for me, particularly in winter. Just being in Scandinavia can have a depressing effect, due to long months of darkness in winter the further north you go. Icelanders, in particular, consume the highest number of antidepressants in the world (OECD, 2013). This can be an incredible shock to students who are new to the environment, whether they have any experience with anxiety and depression or not. Vitamin D or cod liver oil are often recommended in the winter months to offset the effects of the lack of sunlight in Scandinavia.

'Njóti sá er nam': He Who Learns Will Benefit From It

In general, education is very popular in Scandinavia. The number of PhDs doubled in Scandinavia in the 1990s. The Scandinavian countries are among those that spend the most public funds on education in the world. Denmark, Norway and Sweden spend the highest amount on educational institutions per student. Because of this, enrollment rates are high, and more than 60% of young people will attend higher education (Kalpazidou Scmidt, 2010). All of this makes Scandinavia an attractive place for PhDs students to research, especially if they hail from countries with much higher tuition, such as the United States.

Across the Scandinavian countries, almost three-quarters of the population know someone with a physical or mental disability, and more than 70% say they feel at ease with people with disabilities (EORG, 2001). Because of this, it may feel more open and the visitor might be surprised by matter-of-fact or direct questions about disability.

A friend of mine who started her academic journey in the 90s describes the atmosphere as 'a whole different ballgame' for herself as a visually-impaired person. In her experience attending universities in Denmark and Iceland, there has been a huge historical change in the way people with disability are met at the University today. She said 'I am visually impaired and could, before I became legally blind, pass for a non-handicapped person. And I never told anyone about my impairment knowing that in the unlikely event that I received help it would damage my academic career. Back then, I would rather fail exams than get special aid due to the stigma. But much has changed since those times.

Today, there is much more acceptance of disability. There is much more diversity at campus and you are less likely to stick out. Also, having reached the level of a PhD student, my friend feels that she is not so easily dismissed as when she began her university program as an undergraduate.

She pointed out that, of course, 'the trees do not grow into heaven,' as the Danes say, and there is still a fair amount of social awkwardness, physical obstacles and occasional prejudices, but the biggest change is that now you are allowed to address it. Being frank about your disability can earn you respect and help to fill in any blanks in your CV that otherwise could not be explained: It is no longer something you should feel you have to hide or downplay. My friend recommends honesty and claiming your rights. 'Remember that you are not your disability—so try not to get too tangled up in it', she noted.

The United Nations Convention on the Rights of Persons with Disabilities in 2008 mandated a special effort across the UN, which includes all Nordic countries, to change attitudes toward people with disabilities by providing more education and awareness to the public and workplaces, and passing legislation to enforce anti-discrimination (Fisher & Purcal, 2016).

Similarly, all Nordic universities have a general mandate to provide disabled students and staff the conditions that will enable them to actively participate in higher education. Specific types of help for different types of disability are outlined on their websites.

What this means for you as a PhD candidate with a disability is that help is available and you can embrace these opportunities to get the resources you need.

This Is Harder Than I Thought: Diagnosis and Self-care

Healthcare in Scandinavia is socialized, however, doctors may hesitate to prescribe your medications if you are visiting them for the first time (Kristiansen & Pedersen, 2000). If you have already gone through a lengthy diagnosis or a number of prescriptions, make an appointment at your clinic to meet with a doctor when you arrive.

This is determined in slightly different ways in each Nordic country; for example, in Iceland, your clinic is determined by your address, and in Denmark, you are assigned a specific doctor and will go to his or her clinic.

Bring any records you can from your home country or region, as well as your prescriptions, and explain your diagnosis. Ask any questions you have about the healthcare system so that you can feel informed up front.

This way, if you do have an issue later, you can see your doctor and hopefully he or she will be able to help you more quickly. Scandinavia as a whole is very informal, usually operating on a first-name basis, and people value face-to-face meetings to get to know a person over more impersonal forms like e-mail, so it's worth it to make this effort when you arrive. It may save you time getting what you need later.

If you've never been diagnosed, you may also be asked to visit a therapist or other doctor to confirm your diagnosis and, depending on your needs, it may be a long process. Once you have your diagnosis, it's important, like any PhD student, to take care of yourself and do all that you can to get enough sleep, eat well, and exercise (see Chapter 9). If you have medication, make sure you take it. Be aware that Scandinavia has many national holidays in the spring months where doctor's offices and pharmacies are closed, so plan your refills around these days.

Even if you don't need full-time accommodations, consider the more infrequent times when you may need a helping hand, such as during exams. There can be an element of shame associated with having a disability and asking for accommodations, and we often hesitate to ask because we don't want to stand out for the wrong reasons. But you must look at the bigger picture and remember that exams are stressful for everyone. If you can benefit from extra time or some other accommodation, then you owe it to yourself to seek out the environment where you can perform at your best.

A friend who is on the autism spectrum believes that asking for accommodations has made the biggest difference in her academic career. 'I'd never have been so successful at university if I hadn't made use of the support and help offered,' she said. 'I have had great help from the counselors that have helped me get extended exam time, and extended essay deadlines and so on. During exams, I'm in a room with fewer people, and I get to sit in the front row as I feel distracted if I can see the other students.' She recommends that everyone talks to the counselors at their institution and see what support they can offer. Often that support is tailored to your needs and they try as much as they can to make studying easier for those with disabilities.

For another friend of mine, who studies in the Humanities, her diagnosis and self-care is part of a journey which began when she had her first psychotic experience at 19. In the time since, she has earned several other degrees, including BA, a BSc and a MSc with distinction and finally a Master's degree. She is most grateful for the understanding and support she received from her doctors, in her native Iceland and those in Sweden after her studies took her there.

Another source of strength and encouragement for this friend when her illness makes it difficult to continue is her supervisor, whom she describes as 'a mountain of strength.'

I Don't Want Them to Think I'm Crazy: Talking to Your Supervisor

Relationships with supervisors are discussed in Chapters 12 and 13. Here, that relationship will be considered with a focus on disability and support. Your supervisor is your first line of defense. He or she will need to know if you are dealing with any issues that may impact your work, your ability to meet deadlines, etc. It may be your supervisor's first time advising someone with a disability, as PhD candidates with disabilities are still relatively rare. Be ready to communicate your needs and answer questions.

It can be intimidating to speak of these issues with a supervisor, as everyone wants to put their best foot forward and be seen as capable and hardworking. It might be better to think of yourself not as a student approaching a superior, but as a person who is on the path to becoming a peer. Being aware of your needs and communicating them clearly will help your advisor understand, and it speaks highly of your dedication that you want to approach your PhD research as fully equipped as you can be to confront any adversity that may pop up along the way.

Work together with your supervisor to come up with a work plan that fits you. If you need your supervisor to be less hands-on, to allow you space to work without pressure, say so. If you would like your advisor to set a series of deadlines to make sure you are steadily writing, do so. Your supervisor can also help you find the right accommodations to support your work, if you need any.

Winter Is Coming

If you have a physical disability, the winter season may be a particularly difficult time due to icy roads or sidewalks, but public transportation can help you get around. In Iceland, the bus system is privately owned and more expensive, but all buses are equipped with wheelchair lifts or ramps. You can also telephone a taxi company to arrange pickup in a specially equipped van. In the larger Scandinavian countries, newer buses have low floors and wheelchair lifts, as well as other transportation options like trams and the metro system.

It is, however, generally accepted that residents in Scandinavian countries are accustomed to the snow and ice of winter, and so shoveling of sidewalks and public areas can be unreliable. There have been many occasions where I have ended up face down in a snow drift and relied upon the kindness of strangers to get me on my feet again.

If there are days when you can't leave home, embrace online research portals. Search for open access materials on websites like ResearchGate and JSTOR, as well as any websites accessible through your university for more online material. Create a space in your apartment or dorm room for research so you will be less distracted by being at home. That way, you can do some research or source-gathering and not feel disappointed for wasting an entire day because the library was closed, your illness is flaring up, or the weather is too windy to go out.

Chronic Illness: Getting a PhD Without Leaving Your Bed

Of course, some students who have a chronic illness may not be able to take an active part in campus life for long stretches at a time, not just when the weather is bad. A friend with ME/CFS (myalgic encephalomyelitis/chronic fatigue syndrome) points out that living with chronic illness means that you cannot be productive in the conventional meaning of the word; you cannot spend long hours at work and disrespect your body without ill consequences. The stress of 'going forward' on a career path is not a healing state to be in.

On the other hand, research may be just the thing to fill long hours when you cannot exert yourself. A PhD can give you a sense of purpose and kill the boredom of being sick.

In her experience, living with chronic illness means living with an invisible disability. 'It can be hard to set limits when people expect you to participate equally in labor-intensive situations. I fail at that all the time because I want to do my share. I have been fortunate to have a supervisor that is really supportive and tries to understand my illness,' she said, echoing the thoughts of others with disabilities that I spoke to. 'It means taking time to explain your condition, but I really do not know how to do a PhD with a chronic illness without making that effort.'

If you are going to enter a PhD program where you know you may need to take long stretches away from your work, let your supervisor or program heads know as soon as possible. There may be time limits governing the amount of time you can take off, or deadlines by which you must finish your project, but those can vary by institution. Letting the right people know of your situation ahead of time will allow them to prepare to support you in whatever way they can, should you fall ill.

Þetta reddast: It Will Work Out!

Your university or the government in your country of study may have more resources available to you as a PhD student, so be sure to ask your supervisor or at student services for more information. For example, if you are a Schengen Area,[1] European Union (EU) or European Economic Area (EEA)[2] student traveling to another country for your education, you may qualify for a disability pension which can supplement your income if you are unable to work.

Most importantly, know what you need and find out what is available to you. The decision to embark on a PhD is a huge project that requires years of passion and dedication. Because of this, it can be stressful even for those who do not have a disability. Recent studies have shown that half of all PhD students experiences psychological distress; one in three is at risk of a common psychiatric disorder, especially depression (Levecque, Anseel, Beuckelaer, Heyden, & Gisle, 2017).

Begin as you mean to go on. Setting up accommodations and work strategies with your university, and your supervisor in particular, can go a long way to preparing you to succeed. By finding a balance in your needs, your work-family interface, job demands, the supervisor's leadership style, and your perception of a career outside academia can all help mitigate the challenges of pursuing a Nordic PhD as a person with a disability.

Notes

1. The Schengen Area is composed of 26 European states that have officially abolished passport and any other type of border control at their mutual borders.
2. The EEA is an area for non-EU member countries like Iceland and Norway. Although they are not full members, they still follow the same rules and laws as the EU in regards to disability and social welfare.

References

Chen, R. K., Brodwin, M. G., Cardoso, E., & Fong, C. (2002). Attitudes toward people with disabilities in the social context of dating and marriage: A comparison of American, Taiwanese, and Singaporean college students. *Journal of Rehabilitation, 68*(4), 5–11.

European Opinion Research Group (EORG). (2001). *Attitudes of Europeans to disability: Eurobarometer 54.2* (Rep.). Brussels: Author. Retrieved from http://ec.europa.eu/public_opinion/archives/ebs/ebs_149_en.pdf

Fisher, K. R., & Purcal, C. (2016). Policies to change attitudes to people with disabilities. *Scandinavian Journal of Disability Research, 19*(2), 1–14. doi:10.1080/15017419.2016.1222303

Kalpazidou Scmidt, E. (2010). Higher education in Scandinavia. In P. Altbach & J. Forest (Eds.), *International handbook of higher education: Part one: Global themes and contemporary challenges, part two: Regions and countries* (pp. 517–537). Berlin: Springer.

Kristiansen, I. S., & Pedersen, K. M. (2000). Health care systems in the Nordic countries—More similarities than differences? *Tidsskr Nor Laegeforen, 120*(17), 2023–2029.

Levecque, K., Anseel, F., Beuckelaer, A. D., Heyden, J. V., & Gisle, L. (2017). Work organization and mental health problems in PhD students. *Research Policy, 46*(4), 868–879. doi:10.1016/j.respol.2017.02.008

Organisation for Economic Co-operation and Development (OECD). (2013). *Health at a Glance 2013: OECD Indicators* (Rep.). Paris: Author. Retrieved from http://dx.doi.org/10.1787/health_glance-2013-en

Snorri Sturluson. (2014). *The poetic Edda* (C. Larrington, Trans.). Oxford: Oxford University Press.

CHAPTER ELEVEN

Studying with Sensory Processing Disorder

Reframing Disabilities as Strengths

LAURIE PRANGE

Introduction

Every day most people use five senses to navigate the world: sight, smell, hearing, taste, and touch. These influence everything we do and learn. However, in truth, we have eight senses: the vestibular, which is the sense of your head moving in space; proprioceptive, which is the sensation of your muscles and joints in your body moving; and interoception, which is an awareness of your internal organs (Kranowitz, 2005). Most people can filter out all the sensations that continually bombard them. However, many cannot and they have what is referred to as Sensory Processing Disorder (SPD). I have SPD, which means that I struggle to appropriately balance out sensory data from these eight senses. Sometimes I am oversensitive, and at other times I am under-sensitive. My SPD has given me a specific set of needs.

In contemplating further study, I needed to consider a series of questions to determine my fit for doctoral studies. This chapter encourages anyone considering doctoral studies to reflect on these same issues and find an answer that works for you. Applying coping strategies, tailored to my needs, has been the key to my success.

Many people have sensory challenges and the strategies offered in this chapter are not limited to someone with SPD. For example, many people have issues with scents, perhaps because of allergies, and need to think strategically about career choices because of this challenge. Other people have difficulties with chronic pain and require an ergonomic keyboard or standing desk. Other people without SPD may also be extra sensitive to noise or light and struggle with focus, concentration, and productivity, like someone with SPD. The challenge of balancing sensory data in order to focus is more frequent with the increase in open-concept office spaces. This chapter will highlight various strategies developed by psychologists and occupational therapists for people on the autism spectrum and those with SPD that can also benefit those working with, supporting, and supervising an individual with a sensory sensitivity, disability, or disorder.

Sensory Processing Disorder

Sensory Processing Disorder and sensory integration challenges experienced by people on the autism spectrum may be experienced more intensely to the point that the person may behave quite differently from a neurotypical person.

Some disabilities, particularly neurological ones, are not obvious to other people. Many people with SPD are labelled as uptight or overly controlling because of their need to control their environment to ensure sensory stimulation is tolerable (Heller, 2015). Happily, I now recognise my over monitoring of environments as beneficial to *many* workplaces.

Sensory issues are not always obvious to others and may require additional explanation. For example, for most neurotypical people eating involves only the senses of taste and smell, but for someone with auditory issues eating has its challenges with sound, too (Sheahan, 2013). Many aspects of networking as a PhD student involve dining, so it may require taking the time to explain why one may seem uptight, as mentioned above, during social dining events. Students with sensory issues need to be prepared to use extra communication strategies to convey cultural respect and tact when traditional foods are served in situations where they are struggling with sensory integration.

Not everyone with SPD is sensory-sensitive; some under receive information and become sensory seeking, which has its social challenges too. Those who are under sensitive to sensory input may seek out this information in ways that are generally not considered socially acceptable. For example, a tactile seeker may not be able to resist stroking another person's corduroy sweater or furry scarf.

For many people, asking for accommodations at the level of doctoral studies may not strategically be the best choice (Rose, 2008). This is something every student must deliberate in light of his or her own circumstances. While you are a doctoral student, professors are evaluating your potential to join them as a colleague. Unfortunately, with the very high number of available candidates for post-PhD positions, the chance of getting a professorship is as low as one in four (Dehaas, 2014). I did not choose the option of requesting official accommodations because when I first started doctoral studies I was still on my journey of revealing my condition to others and navigating their response. Many things that would have needed an accommodation in undergraduate programs were no longer issues at the doctoral level because of the nature of doctoral studies and the utilization of the strategies discussed below.

Being a Researcher with SPD

Having SPD is like living beside a hospital. In a few weeks, most people would stop noticing the ambulance sirens. Those with SPD, on the other hand, will hear sirens as brand new every time, flooding the body with endorphins. However, being unable to adjust to stimuli is an opportunity. Over time, I would start to notice patterns in siren frequency (to use the hospital analogy) that no one else would. I would note, for example, that ambulances went out on call more often on Friday than Saturday night and that the full moon resulted in more call outs. Noticing, analyzing, and recording information to identify patterns of behaviour is also a key skill for a researcher. The mind of someone with SPD is primed for the observation and pattern mapping required for advanced research.

The doctoral-level learning environment for someone with SPD can be a favorable environment. The apprenticeship model means that you can choose your supervisor and committee and, unlike a bachelor's program, stick with the same teacher from semester to semester. By working with the same faculty members over several years it is easier to hear and listen, as you are more attuned to the body language of that person. When a brain never gets used to stimuli, minimizing any changes will improve your chances for success.

As a doctoral student, pursuing new and potentially triggering experiences and environments, required me to adjust for my SPD. Part of my doctoral program required short periods of residency in Denmark. Moving to a new continent was like entering an emotional and physical hurricane. Adjusting to a new country when you are not neurotypical requires self-awareness. Seeing, hearing, and feeling everything in exquisite detail, means everything is not just new and exciting, it is an existential crisis.

During my first residency period in Denmark, I initially pretended to be neurotypical. I did not budget the extra time needed to adjust and did not bring my toolkit to classes. It was a mistake. My difficulties adjusting caused me to begin to worry. What if I could not complete an intensive, immersive campus experience again? What if I could not complete a degree program with mandatory residencies?

Determining Your Working Style

The PhD environment is ideal for someone with SPD. Small, intimate classes in a seminar set-up worked very well for me. Some of my classes in my undergraduate studies were as large as 500 students and it was nearly impossible for me to function with so much noise and body language. However, in classes of just a few students, I was able to focus and learn better than at any other stage of my academic career.

In Scandinavia, courses at the PhD level are taught in intensive time blocks and are often only five days long. These classes require extensive reading and writing by students beforehand. Discussions and presentations are concentrated into this short time. This can be an ideal learning environment—you can read and write according to your schedule, and then focus only on visual and auditory input during class time. Not having to switch back and forth between learning strategies and data input can improve your ability to learn successfully and have a positive learning experience overall.

Having a Plan for Potential Problems

Classroom time can be a challenge. Quickly identifying what are the triggers to sensory overload is critical to implementing the appropriate coping strategies. In sharing my methods below, I offer examples that worked for me. Every student will need to find those coping strategies that suit them and their own specific needs. I also recommend working with an Occupational Therapist and Psychologist familiar with sensory integration problems.

My most important strategy for social environments is the use of therapy glasses. In private spaces, I also rely on noise-cancelling devices. My therapy glasses have a blue tinted lens that reduces the fluorescent lighting common in university classrooms. Light overstimulation for many people with SPD can lead to a manic state and make it difficult to pay attention (Henriksen et al., 2016).

I own three pairs of glasses with differing levels of blue tint. The lightest tint pair is in a stylish frame, and I often will wear them in social settings. Few people have ever commented on the blue tint. I also use these glasses in a work setting where I want to make sure I do not become over stimulated, such as formal meetings where a computer projector will be shining brightly. If a classmate I did not know inquired about my glasses and I did not feel comfortable explaining SPD, I would say that I had eye fatigue from using computers. It is important to remember that you do not need to explain yourself.

In addition to using lenses to reduce visual sensory stimulation, I also use several devices to minimize auditory input. In most stores that sell a large selection of bedding, you can purchase a variety of white noise machines. Many people use white noise machines to improve sleep hygiene. Individuals with SPD often use these devices in their social spaces at home or offices at work for the same calming effect. I own a small portable one that has traveled with me to Denmark for my short residencies. There are also a variety of apps available now that may be far more portable. Using a fan often works well too.

I also own several noise-cancelling earmuffs. These devices are made for people working in loud construction sites and factories. Some people also like to use earplugs, while others find they need a combination of earplugs and noise-cancelling earmuffs to focus successfully. Noise-cancelling earmuffs have been used successfully for years with students who struggle to concentrate in school, such as those with ADHD. It has become common to see someone in a university library wearing a pair. Recently, manufacturers have started marketing earplugs with a metal core, which are said to reduce noise better than the foam and wax ones.

For those people with SPD who are tactile sensitive, there is the Wilbarger Protocol, using a surgical brush to promote sensory integration by brushing the skin (Headley et al., 2015). Many people with SPD and autism pack a Wilbarger brush in a kit to go to class or social events along with their blue-tinted glasses and earplugs. I have not found this strategy works for me, so I instead dress in ways to cover up as much skin as possible and always bring a large, light scarf to add layers to minimize sensory data input by touch. Preparing a package for studies and networking events will help you start your first semester off as smoothly as possible.

Another tool used by many people with SPD is a weighted sensory vest or weighted blanket, made famous by Temple Grandin (2015). While I do not have a weighted vest, I have often used a heated therapy pad around my neck while typing at my computer. I also own a weighted blanket, which I have found will calm me down so well that my Fitbit registers me as in Light Sleep during use despite being wide awake! An alternative to weighted items is to wear compression clothes. Compression garments can include knee-high socks as well as items designed for women to improve their figure. For days that required an extreme amount of concentration, particularly professional conferences, I usually wear at least one compression item to help manage my sensory integration.

Utilising the Work Environment

Doctoral students are valued members of the university community. In Scandinavia, doctoral students are considered employees of the universities. As such, they have access to the departmental staff lounge, which allows them to bring their own food or drink, which gets around any food aversion for people with SPD. Doctoral students also have nearly complete control over their own schedules, like faculty members. The day before a departmental event that I knew would be overly stimulating, with lots of noise and tastes, I would do my best to have a very quiet day. Danes, and Scandinavians generally, value quiet moments in their lives (Wiking, 2016). No one will find it unusual if you were to schedule quiet days before a major social event.

Scandinavians take ergonomics seriously (Jensen, 1997). Health in the workplace is a responsibility for all employers, and the university environment is no different. On my first visit, I was shown my shared office with its motorized stand-up desk. I was sure a mistake had been made. But, the university had a policy that ensured every employee would eventually have a full-sized stand-up desk. As my departmental secretary explained, these desks cost the same as regular non-motorized desks and make it easier for people to move offices as well as to tailor the working arrangement for varying heights. I noticed an immediate difference to how I felt typing at my computer when I was able to adjust my chair and desk height to perfectly suit my 5′3″ frame. With the emphasis on good design, ergonomics is a high priority across most Nordic countries. Discussing sound design is such a common topic for small talk that you may find yourself discussing favorite chair designs during a class break.

Reaching Out for Help

Despite well thought-through plans and a toolkit, sometimes sensory overload may still be a challenge. During my third residency in Denmark, I found myself struggling to write and sometimes even to leave my studio apartment. I contacted Rachel Schneider, author of the blog *Coming to my Senses* (http://comingtosenses.blogspot.ca) and fellow adult SPDer. Via e-mail, we discussed what I was experiencing and identified that because of the stress of doctoral work, I needed to minimize sensory input even more than I had before.

We also reviewed several of the coping strategies she covers in her book (Schneider, 2016) to identify any I had not yet tried. So, for a while, I switched to writing in my studio apartment in an unusual arrangement. I turned off all the lights, put on a fan with a different pitch from my white noise machine, put on comfortable pajamas, and climbed into bed. I typed on my computer lying on my back with the laptop on my stomach. Sometimes I slightly propped my head up to see the screen, but most of the time I laid my head flat on the mattress and closed my eyes as I typed.

I also discussed my challenges with my supervisor and he proposed an alternative to writing that used the way I would go into a slight state of mania during public presentations. On a monthly basis, departmental faculty would meet in a seminar room to present and discuss their latest research. My supervisor arranged for me to start regularly presenting to this group. We recorded these presentations and the transcripts from these talks became first drafts of chapters. Initially, I thought it was the act of talking aloud and hearing my voice that helped me get unstuck. Over time, I realized it was also the bright computer projector, watching the audience's body language, and the pacing I did that together gave me the positive sensory input and integration I needed to organize thoughts as I was working on various parts of my dissertation. Using public presentations as a means to get unstuck with one's writing is often recommended to extroverts and one that continues to work well for me. The first draft of this chapter was written by video chatting with a friend and transcribing the call.

Conclusion

Many people are unaware that there is a range of options for people with SPD to improve their doctoral studies. You do not have to rely on willpower to control sensory overload and integration. Willpower should be the last option when managing sensory input, not the first. Tweaks in one's environment, toolkits, and strategies, can go a long way in making being a PhD student in Scandinavia, or anywhere, a pleasurable, rewarding, and ultimately successful experience despite living, studying, and writing with SPD.

References

Dehaas, J. (2014, May 22). When Ph.D.s realize they won't be professors: Young academics struggle with the transition from school to work. *Maclean's Magazine*. Retrieved from http://www.macleans.ca/work/jobs/phds-realize-they-wont-be-professors-now-what/

Grandin, T. (2015). *Temple talks about autism and sensory issues: The world's leading expert on autism shares her advice and experiences*. Arlington, TX: Sensory World.

Headley, J. A., Ammermann, K., Annable, J., Bogino, C., Brosemer, J., Day, R., … Kurzac, E. (2015). *Awareness & perceptions of sensory processing disorders & sensory diets in day care facilities*. Utica, NY: Utica College.

Heller, S. (2015). *Uptight & off center: How sensory processing disorder throws adults off balance & how to create stability*. Delray Beach, FL: Symmetry Publishing.

Henriksen, T. E., Skrede, S., Fasmer, O. E., Schoeyen, H., Leskauskaite, I., Bjorke-Bertheussen, J. J., … Lund, A. (2016). Blue-blocking glasses as additive treatment for mania: A randomized placebo-controlled trial. *Bipolar Disorders, 18*(3), 221–232.

Jensen, P. L. (1997). Can participatory ergonomics become 'the way we do things in this firm': The Scandinavian approach to participatory ergonomics. *Ergonomics, 40*(10), 1078–1087.

Kranowitz, C. S. (2005). *The out-of-sync child: Recognizing and copying with sensory integration dysfunction*. New York, NY: Berkley Publishing Group.

Rose, S. F. (2008). Disability and the academic job market. *Disability Studies Quarterly, 28*(3). Retrieved from http://dsq-sds.org/article/view/111/111#top.

Schneider, R. (2016). *Making sense: A guide to sensory issues*. Arlington, TX: Sensory World.

Sheahan, B. (2013, Spring). Listen to your food: Focus on diet. *Sensory Focus Magazine*.

Wiking, M. (2016). *The little book of hygge: The Danish way to live well*. London: Penguin.

PART FOUR

A Matter of Relationships

CHAPTER TWELVE

The Evolving Relationship Between Supervisor and PhD Student

LOUISE FLOOR FRELLSEN

Introduction

There are three crucial components that will help you get through your PhD: Your personal engagement, your interest in the project, and your supervisor. A good supervisor can give you the first two. Any researcher who really cares about their work can make a project interesting and make you excited about it. A supervisor who respects you will also make you want to work hard, simply because you feel like you're making a real difference.

Every supervisor is different. Some will want to micromanage and have a meeting every day. Others may just want you to run your own project and will only talk to you if you are stuck. Some have many students to keep track of and seem to barely have any time for your project. None of this is what makes a good or a bad supervisor the question is, 'what is a good supervisor for *you*?' If you have several PhD project opportunities to choose from, this might be a thing to consider in advance. However, it can be difficult to know if you will work well with your supervisor until you have tried it. In any case, it is worthwhile to get involved in what shape and form your supervision takes.

This chapter discusses the relationship between supervisors and their students, how it evolves in the course of a PhD, and what you can do to make sure that your supervision takes the form that works best for you. The following sections investigate the role of the supervisor and the progression of the relationship with them chronologically in the doctoral process. Your supervisor is an important factor throughout your project, but what they contribute to your project changes as your experience and knowledge grow. By being aware of your own progress and where you need guidance the most, you can make sure that you benefit optimally from having a dedicated mentor. Even the best supervisors won't know exactly what you need unless you know and learn how to tell them.

The Beginning of the Project

When you start a PhD in Scandinavia, you are hired as a researcher. This means that you are at the same time a student and part of the staff (part of what Carsten Lund Pedersen refers to as 'boundary spanning' in Chapter 15). If you come directly from university studies, you might still feel like a student when you begin your PhD. Over time you will transition from being a student, who needs to figure out how everything works, to being a full-fledged member of your research team, with your own plans and ideas for what to do. Just as you will be changing in this period, so too will the relationship with your supervisor. This is natural, but it can be difficult to transition from simply following instructions to sometimes telling your supervisor that you disagree on how to proceed.

Some prospective PhD students have the opportunity to meet their supervisors in advance and develop the project description together, some continue where they did their final university project, and some enter into something completely new. No matter what, you are going to be dependent on your supervisor in the beginning of the project. In this initial stage of the PhD, there might be substantial micromanaging of the work. Your supervisor tells you what to do, you work on this, and then come back to get more directions. This is a productive way to start the project. You are not expected to be able to work on your own from day one, and guiding you into the field is exactly what your supervisor is there for. He or she is the one with the initial vision of where this project is going as well as the one who knows the field and relevant literature. At this point of the project the supervisor knows most as they have more experience. Your supervisor gives you more attention and time than later on. Enjoy this and take advantage of the fact that somebody wants to share their knowledge with you. In the beginning, the relationship with your supervisor will be more like that of a student and teacher.

In Scandinavia, your supervisor is not only your boss. Academic relationships in the Scandinavian culture are not particularly formal and the majority of companies, including the universities, have a flat organizational structure (Eriksen, Kruse, & Larsen, 2006; Warner-Søderholm, 2012). People treat each other as people. Titles aren't important on a day-to-day basis, and if you bring them up, people might perceive you as arrogant. In practice, this means that even if you start with very limited knowledge of the field, your thoughts on what to do in the project are valued. Even if your supervisor is an established researcher, think of him or her primarily as another person.

The ideal relationship with a supervisor in Scandinavia is professional and collegial—but it can also be a friendship with room for sharing thoughts and experiences from outside the workplace. By talking about subjects other than your research, you get a better understanding of each other as people. Similarly, knowing and respecting that you both have a life outside of work is important to maintain a healthy work-life-balance that will benefit your project and long-term research output.

The Evolution of Supervisor Meetings and Multiple Supervisors

Having regular scheduled meetings with your supervisor is vital. How often they occur depends on you, your supervisor, and what kind of project you do. Regular meetings are an essential way of getting an overview, and keeping track of where you are in your project.

Just like everything else in your project, the nature of the meetings will change over time. In the beginning, your supervisor is taking charge. Your meetings will consist of you relating what you have done and your supervisor instructing you in what to do for the next meeting. As you get more acquainted with your material, however, more of the responsibility for the meetings will become yours. You will not only explain what you have been doing, but will also come with suggestions for how to proceed. Once you start taking charge of your own work, your supervisor will start keeping less track of your project and spend more of their energy on other things—possibly to the point where you will need to remind them what you are in the middle of and why. As your responsibility in your project develops, your supervisors might become less active towards staying updated on your work. At this point, it is your task to make sure that supervisor meetings continue to be held, even if less frequently and on a less regular schedule than in the initial phase of your project.

The number of supervisors assigned to a project can vary. In some cases, you will have a single supervisor, but often you will have one or more co-supervisors. The benefit of having more supervisors is to have different perspectives, and each of the supervisors is typically involved at different levels. Some will give you advice on a day-to-day basis, others less frequently, and others you might only see at the supervisor meetings. Even the supervisors you only see rarely can provide valuable input. Diversity in viewpoints towards your project is healthy, even if you might need or choose to ignore some of the advice you receive. Also, having to sum up all of your work and giving an overview to someone who isn't as deeply involved as yourself is a healthy exercise that may help you to see your project and work in a broader perspective. Beware that different supervisors may be involved at different levels at different stages of your project, so make sure to review how you use and interact with your supervisors as your project progresses.

Transitioning to Knowing What the Right Next Step Is

Once you gain some experience in your field, you typically know the group you work in, you have gotten a good grasp of your methods and theories, and you will begin to form your own visions for your project. When you reach this point depends on you, on your project, and on the field; it can take anywhere between a few weeks or until you are more than halfway into your project. When you get there, explore your ideas with your supervisor. It might be intimidating to transition from following instructions, to discussing and disagreeing. But do it. It is beneficial for you, and chances are that your supervisor will be happy to see that you are growing as a researcher. Even if you do not end up pursuing all your ideas and suggestions, you will be part of a professional discussion and will learn from that. This might be the point where you learn most about how to plan research, think ahead, and become more efficient with your time (Ehiobuche, Tu, & Justus, 2012).

Your supervisor knows a lot about the field you are working in, but slowly you become the expert on what *you* are working on. Your supervisor may have several students, they might teach classes, and also conduct their own research. Even though they have more overall knowledge, particularly about the methods of research and the requirements of a doctorate, you are likely, at this stage, to know what next step would be the best. You might still have doubts and questions, and that is why you still need your supervisor—not to give you the ideas, but to help figure out which of *your* ideas are best. If you think that parts of your research are ready to be published, then say so and discuss that possibility with your supervisor.

During the Writing Phase

Even if you are the most pro-active and well-organized PhD student, chances are that you will do a substantial amount of thesis writing towards the end of the project. At this point, talk to your supervisor about your thesis outline. In what order should the chapters be written and what should they contain? Breaking it down and discussing it with your supervisor will make the task less daunting. If you need references on a specific problem or topic, your supervisor can help by pointing you in the right direction. Similarly, you can ask him or her to read a chapter or a few sections that you are in doubt about, or if you want general feedback about style and level of detail. Make sure to still have supervisory meetings during this crucial time. It will help you maintain an overview, and see how much progress you actually make. If deadlines work well for you, have your supervisor help you break up the task, by sending chapters to him or her one at a time for specific deadlines along the way. The thesis is a major part of the doctoral degree, and shepherding you successfully through the writing process is a major part of the supervisor's purpose; rely on their advice and guidance, which is based on years of experience. Advice on when and how to write the thesis can be found in Chapter 5.

Nearing the End and Being in Charge

Once you near the end of your project, you have become an expert in your area of study. You know what you are doing and where you are going. You can pull your own weight, and that feels great. But this doesn't mean you don't need your supervisor anymore. You can always benefit from somebody to spar with (Peluchette & Jeanquart, 2000) and you are lucky to have somebody who knows exactly what you're talking about and who is invested in the project. No matter how self-sufficient you feel, and how great it feels that you can run your own project, don't waste the opportunity to get input.

Maintain a regular meeting schedule, chat over coffee or show up at the office when you have questions. It is not important how you do it, as long as you maintain the contact. You might not *need* it, but you still learn from it. Remember that no matter how busy your supervisor is, you never have to feel guilty to approach them; guiding you to be a researcher is an important part of their job.

Sometimes you disagree with your supervisors, and other times your supervisors disagree with each other. They may change their minds and make you confused about which direction they are headed in. At times like that, and throughout your entire project, remember: It is *your* project, and you have the right to shape it the way you want it to be.

Final Thoughts

In the beginning, it might not feel like your project. You might feel that it is your supervisor's project that you just happen to help out with. But as you go along, you get more attached to the study. You will be the one who spends most time on it. You will become the expert. It will eventually become *your* project. At some point, you might worry that you are not ready and not skilled enough. Your supervisor's goal is to teach you to do your own research and manage a project. Shape the project and take charge by letting your supervisors know what you want to happen. What you think is interesting, important and possible. When you tell your supervisors what you want, you are not doing anything wrong. You are telling them that this is *your* project and that you care about it. You are showing that you are ready to take your place among equals in the academic community.

References

Ehiobuche, C., Tu, H.-W., & Justus, B. (2012). Dialogue as a tool for teaching and learning of entrepreneurship. *Proceedings of ASBBS, 19*(1), 300–309. Retrieved from http://asbbs.org/files/ASBBS2012V1/PDF/E/EhiobucheC.pdf

Eriksen, T. T., Kruse, M., & Larsen, G. (2006). The Scandinavian way. *Futureorientation, 5.* Retrieved from http://cifs.dk/publications/scenario-magazine/2006/fo-2006/futureorientation-52006/the-scandinavian-way/

Peluchette, J. van Eck, & Jeanquart, S. (2000). Professionals' use of different mentor sources at various career stages: Implications for career success. *The Journal of Social Psychology, 140*(5), 549–564. doi:10.1080/00224540009600495

Warner-Søderholm, G. (2012). Culture matters: Norwegian cultural identity within a Scandinavian context. *SAGE Open, 2*(4), 1–12. doi:10.1177/2158244012471350

CHAPTER THIRTEEN

You, Your Supervisor, and the Importance of *fika*

BETHANNE PAULSRUD

Introduction

As a PhD student, you will form many new relationships with individuals who will play an important role in your academic life—none as important as your supervisor. Prior to your position as a doctoral student, you may have had other roles of responsibility, such as a junior lecturer, a teacher in school, or an employee in a business or lab. When you start your PhD programme, you might feel as though you are ten years old again, needing someone to guide you through the complexities of academic life and to raise you to become a full-fledged researcher. While your supervisor will guide you, they are not there to parent you.

This chapter will help you understand how to navigate your relationship with your supervisor in the best possible manner for both of you. The chapter offers guidance on the initial stages of supervision as well as on the regular scheduled meetings that are part of doctoral supervision, helping you to navigate both expectations and responsibilities. Cultivating a positive relationship with your supervisor involves planning and preparation, but also an occasional cup of coffee, what is known in Sweden as *fika*.

You and Your Supervisor

In the Beginning

How you are advised during your PhD studies can vary greatly from one country to another. In North America, for example, you have a committee with several advisors, involved in different stages of your work or with different aspects of your studies (Semenza, 2005). In Australia and the UK, PhD students are not obliged to take formal courses, making the relationship with the supervisors even more crucial as the entire thesis is dependent on research guided by the supervisor (Heath, 2002).

In Nordic doctoral programmes, students tend to study and work with the same supervisor during the entire project. They often have two or three co-supervisors, depending on the programme. I had one supervisor from my department and a second from another department in a field relevant for my research project; and each supervisor had equal duties as far as their interaction with me. Some colleagues had one principal supervisor from their departments, and also a second supervisor whom they met less frequently. Your supervisor may be appointed by your department, based on expertise or time available (remember this is a job for them!), or you may have chosen to apply under a particular academic. Each Nordic country differs slightly in this aspect of doctoral study. My first supervisor was assigned to me before I started my studies, and then I happened to meet another well-known researcher at a national conference, in my role as a junior lecturer at another university. Making contact with him and describing my upcoming PhD project helped pave the way for him to become my second supervisor. Even if a supervisor is assigned to you, it is possible to get involved in the assignment and arrangement of your supervisory team.

Your Relationship

Whether you are conducting independent research or participating in a larger study, writing a dissertation is a tough and often lonely job—requiring all the encouragement you can get. Your supervisor is a vital source of support. Earning a PhD ultimately comes down to your own hard work, but 'the *relationship* that doctoral students develop with their advisors is crucial to their success in completing their graduate degree' (Barnes, 2009, p. 324). The supervisor can make or break a PhD student (Lee, 2008). Unfortunately, horror stories about supervisors abound in the world of PhD studies, and changing supervisor once your project has started is in most cases neither desirable nor possible. So, it is in your best interest to cultivate that relationship well.

Developing a good supervisor relationship right from the start is a key ingredient of your chances of completing the degree. A large study of US university STEM (Science, Technology, Engineering, and Mathematics) PhD students found that poor relationships with supervisors were a crucial factor in PhD dropout, especially among female students (Ruud, Saclarides, George-Jackson, & Lubienski, 2016). Several typical problem areas can jeopardise the student-supervisor relationship, including students and supervisors lacking agreement on how to set goals and how to measure them, students *and* supervisors not meeting their deadlines for submitting work or responding to work, and students left floundering with few concrete directives (Wellington, 2010). Most of these problems can be avoided with simple planning and an awareness of the key factors to the success of managing your supervisor and your supervision.

Supervision: Making the Most of It

Planning Meetings

The first question is simple: how often will you and your supervisor meet? This may be regulated by your department, dictated by your supervisor's other engagements, decided by your own field work plans, and more. But early on, you need to sit down with your supervisor and make a general plan for the next years of your doctoral studies. The frequency of supervision can and should change over the course of your studies (Heath, 2002). Wellington (2010, p. 65) offers this piece of advice:

> In the early stages of research more frequent contact is needed when the focus is being sharpened, plans are being laid and ground rules are being set. At later stages, data collection for example, the meeting frequency may be less. In the final phases, for example in finishing the writing, meetings will be largely about feedback and formative assessment of written work and will be of a different kind and frequency. All through the phases of the doctoral journey, these issues need to be jointly negotiated and mutually agreed. (Wellington, 2010)

You will not be able to schedule every session for the entire doctoral period, but discuss the different stages (see Chapter 12) and make estimates of when you need more contact. Regular, frequent contact has been shown to keep PhD students on track: 'Candidates in the sciences have more frequent meetings with their supervisors than do those in the humanities and social sciences,' Heath notes, '[and] they publish more papers and give more oral presentations such as seminars' (2002, p. 49). This is especially important if you will be writing a compilation thesis based on several published journal articles, as you need to keep a tight schedule.

Expectations

Besides knowing when you will meet your supervisor, you both need to be clear about what will actually happen at those meetings, as well as in between them. Find out what your supervisor's expectations and experiences are (Barnes, 2009). Have a specific discussion early in your PhD programme on exactly how each of you envision your supervision sessions. Some supervisors appreciated their students' dedication to completing their degrees in a timely fashion while others highly valued their students' participation in the department activities (Barnes, 2009). Ask your supervisor how he or she has previously worked with her PhD students, what expectations they have and how they see your role as a student. Mutual understanding of expectations is a vital part of your work.

Think about how you work and what kinds of deadlines you need. Late in my own doctoral studies, I learned that the supervisor of one of my new PhD colleagues made it clear that the expectation was a short written report of activities as well as at least a short draft of a section of her thesis every week. While this may seem like a big burden, the regularity of producing text and the accountability to the supervisor would have suited me well. Do you work well with many small deadlines or fewer larger ones? How does your supervisor prefer to receive texts: short ones very often or longer ones less often? Consider your strengths and weaknesses as well as work style. You and your supervisor may be different in these regards, so describing your own stance will be helpful.

Consider your expectations of the imagined role your supervisor will play in your doctoral journey. A supervisor needs to take on many roles: a mentor, a psychologist and an academic (Ohlin, 2013). Your supervisor may be trying to find the right balance between those three and needs to be clear about the plan of action for your thesis work, as well as be aware of your expectations. Use your self-knowledge to guide your supervisor on what you expect from her.

Be Prepared

Be prepared every time you meet your supervisor. Do what you agreed to do at the last session and update your supervisor before the meeting to let him or her know what you want to cover in the upcoming session. Be specific with your questions or concerns, go through them point by point. Send the texts your supervisor needs well in advance. Ask your supervisor how much time he or she needs to read a draft and respect that time limit. If you have not managed to do what you planned at the previous session, make your supervisor aware of this ahead of time. If you planned to discuss your analysis of some of your data, but you did not have time to start the analysis, you may feel that you need to reschedule until you have other topics or questions to cover. But even if you did not manage to finish the entire analysis, or got stock in your interpretation of the data, bring this to the supervisor meeting for a discussion. Part of research is to get stuck and then find solutions and ways out, which is better done with your supervisor than alone.

During the Supervision Meeting

Having expectations for the supervision meeting is important in managing your time together. There are guidelines, or ground rules, for supervision during the actual meeting to help ensure a productive session: for example, the supervisor should not allow interruptions during meetings with the student, such as answering phone calls or knocks on the door, (except in the case of emergency). The supervisor should not cut the meetings short once the time and agenda have been mutually decided. The supervisor should not regularly postpone or reschedule meetings, but should stick to the agreed schedule, (again, unless there is an emergency). The supervisor and the student should agree on the frequency of the meetings according to the current phase of your project (Wellington, 2010).

While these ground rules apply to your supervisor, you also have responsibilities during the session. Take notes or record your session when you meet as you may not remember as much as you think you will. Many of my PhD colleagues found that a combination of recording with a phone or recording device and writing notes was the best solution. That way, after the meeting they could double check the details of discussions and decisions. At the end of each meeting, make a plan with your supervisor about what will be done next, write this down as a list of tasks, and send it to your supervisor so that you both have the documentation.

Bear in mind that the relationship with your supervisor will develop over the course of your PhD studies. As the Chapter 12 author writes, while you may feel like a complete novice at the beginning of your studies, eventually you will become the expert in your topic of study.

Language Help?

Doing research for your doctoral degree can involve sheer messiness in many areas of your work (Wellington, 2010). Experiments can go wrong, field work can be unpredictable, and results may be unexpected. However, messiness should not apply to your writing. Many PhD students in Scandinavia write in English, which in most cases is not their native language. Whether you write in English or a Nordic language (or even another language), seek editing help elsewhere, *as your supervisor is not your language editor*. Use grammar and spell check functions on every text before you submit it to your supervisor for feedback. Drafts full of poor grammar and typos move the focus from the actual content, which is your research. Your university will have a language support centre, but you can also enlist PhD colleagues to act as peer reviewers for language. If you help each other, your supervisors can focus on the content of your research rather than on language editing. See if your university offers a short course in academic writing in English, as many universities do.

Think Outside the Box!

Even though you need to plan ahead and to be prepared, allow yourself the freedom to occasionally think outside the box when it comes to supervision. If you have more than one supervisor, meet them together sometimes and individually at other times. Consider having supervision over lunch or going to a conference together to discuss your study in relation to current research. One former PhD colleague regularly has supervision at her supervisor's cottage in the countryside. They find that a whole day uninterrupted by office clamour works better for both of them.

Do not underestimate the power of *fika*. In Swedish, *fika* means having a cup of coffee and perhaps a biscuit (Brones & Kindvall, 2015). Although *fika* does not have an exact equivalent in other Nordic languages, the informal ritual is surely recognisable across contexts. Think English afternoon tea, but on a much smaller scale, and indeed with more regularity:

> The coffee break in Sweden is an important social gathering, a time to talk about what one is working on or doing. Management and employees sit together and drink coffee and eat cookies, sweet rolls, or cake, and not showing up is considered impolite. (Carr & Robinowitz, 2001, p. 148)

In your new life as PhD student, *fika* can play a key role anywhere in Scandinavia. In between more formal supervision sessions, *fika* can be a wonderful way to informally chat about what is going on. If you and your supervisor both have offices in the same department, create opportunities to talk regularly over a cup of coffee. These brief, casual conversations can not only help keep you focused, allow you to ask minor questions or even share small victories and sorrows from your field work, but also deepen your relationship with your supervisor.

Conclusion

Just like a tête-à-tête over coffee requires two talkers, a good supervision session demands two eager, informed and prepared discussants. To create this, you must first make sure that right from the beginning of your PhD studies you get off to a good start by establishing a positive and open relationship. Maintain this up with clear expectations and responsibility in preparation and follow-up, and remember that you are aiming to create a long professional relationship that will not only help you attain your goal of earning your PhD, but that may also offer many invaluable chats over a cup of coffee.

References

Barnes, B. J. (2009). The nature of exemplary doctoral advisors' expectations and the ways they may influence doctoral ersistence. *Journal of College Student Retention: Research, Theory & Practice, 11*(3), 323–343.

Brones, A., & Kindvall, J. (2015). *Fika: The art of the Swedish coffee break, with recipes for pastries, breads, and other treats.* Berkeley, CA: Ten Speed Press.

Robinowitz, C. J & Carr, L. W. (2001). *Modern-day Vikings: A practical guide to interacting with the Swedes.* Yarmounth, Me.: Intercultural Press.

Heath, T. (2002). A quantitative analysis of PhD students' views of supervision. *Higher Education Research & Development, 21*(1), 41–53.

Lee, A. (2008). How are doctoral students supervised? Concepts of doctoral research supervision. *Studies in Higher Education, 33*(3), 267–281.

Ohlin, C. (2013). *Relationell handledning?: Reflektioner kring handledning av internationella doktorander i Sverige.* Kristianstad: Kristianstad University Press.

Ruud, C. M., Saclarides, E. S., George-Jackson, C. E., & Lubienski, S. T. (2016). Tipping points. *Journal of College Student Retention: Research, Theory & Practice, 1*(1), 1–22.

Semenza, G. M. C. (2005). *Graduate study for the twenty-first century: How to build an academic career in the humanities.* New York, NY: Palgrave Macmillan.

Wellington, J. (2010). *Making supervision work for you: A student's guide.* London: Sage Publications.

CHAPTER FOURTEEN

Parental Leave During Your PhD

Planning, Plotting and Passing!

NATASHA A. WEBSTER

Introduction

As a newcomer to Sweden, I was shocked by the blunt advice I received from senior researchers encouraging PhD candidates to start their families during their PhD studies. 'There's no better time,' so many said. Yet this was the complete opposite of advice I had heard in North America. PhD candidates in Sweden, and other Scandinavian countries, enjoy many benefits of the welfare state and may even receive 'top-ups' through their positions as employees of a university. (For those working on research grants or in post-doctoral grants employment status can be precarious and these benefits vary.) As such, advice from senior researchers that the PhD is a good time to start a family is quite doable in the Scandinavian context.

The advice that follows is drawn my own experience as a working mother while doing my PhD in Sweden. During my candidacy, I took a total of 27 months of parental leave following the birth of my two children and as a post-doctoral researcher I continue to enjoy a 15% workload (and pay) reduction as my youngest is still less than 8 years old. The advice presented in this chapter applies across many scenarios you might find yourself in.

Planning Parent Leave Is a Career Strategy

Parenting has been shown to be a key obstacle in achieving long term success in academia, especially for female, early career researchers. A recent study shows that the impact of having a baby is the equivalent of approximately three academic publications or other equivalent merits (Klocker & Drozdzewski, 2012). In the context of increasing neo-liberal university matrices, the 'publish and perish' agenda is increasingly pertinent to early career researchers, who are often in the young family stages (Drozdzewski & Robinson 2015; Gill & Donaghue 2016; Hawkins, Manzi, & Ojeda, 2014). However, links between family life and success in academia are increasingly important to early career researchers. Getting the best out of your childcare options and striking a good work-life balance will benefit your career potential, help you finish on time and in good relations with your department.

The openness towards family life in Scandinavia can often be different from other countries (Caretta & Webster, 2016). This stems from the strong protections afforded by the welfare states that provide some of the world's best family benefits and also from the strong cultural support for work-family balance. Due to the generosity of parental benefits and general positivity towards becoming a parent during your studies, there are many issues to take into account throughout your time as working parent and researcher. It is important to strike a balance between what works for your family while creating a functional research plan.

Parental Leave in the Scandinavian System

In Scandinavian systems, parental leave is given to benefit the child and to promote gender equality—not to benefit the employer. This may be a slight oversimplification, but the system is focused differently than elsewhere. As a result, the options available are designed to balance your needs, your children's and then your employer's.

Scandinavian welfare systems often include generous parental leave systems. These systems are based on residency and not on employment status. Your entitlements will be based on jurisdiction and residential status. In Sweden, for example, parental leave can include 480 days of paid leave which can be taken at various percentages and pay scales. Leave is done in days—not weeks, months or years—so always be thinking in the day time scale. Parental leave in Sweden can be taken up until the child is eight years old and there are many different kinds of support—child allowances, equity bonuses and multiple types of allowances for children with disabilities. Rainbow families and non-normative family structures also receive the same supports from the government. In some instances, newcomers to Sweden will be granted parental leave upon arrival if their child is under age eight (this can be important for partners who follow their spouses).

Following the initial baby stage, universal child care systems are available for children over the age of one until they are ready to begin school around age seven. Child care services such as nurseries are available to all children, over 1 year, regardless of parent's employment status with varying rules. All of this means that finding a work-life balance as a PhD candidate is possible within the highly functional but complex welfare state, but it does mean that there is a lot more to consider when weighing the different options.

The combination of good child care, flexible work structures and affordability of the public services is designed for you to find balances that work for you to have a family and a career. How you plan your child care options will shape how you do research and build your networks within your field. This applies whether you are a man or woman, as both fathers and mothers in a Scandinavian setting will be expected to take leave as well as be involved in the different kinds of care as their children grow. Gender inequalities certainly exist in Scandinavia, and some departments will be better than others at addressing these. As a general rule, having a family in Scandinavia will not require the 'invisibility' strategies adopted by many academics in other places. On the contrary, beyond planning for your leave and balancing childcare within a work-life balance, directly communicating with your workplace is essential. This will require open communication with your respective departments and colleagues. Socially speaking, family life is highly valued and not taking leave or building pathways into family time would be considered odd by your colleagues, although how you do it is entirely up to you.

The First Year of Leave

Starting a family will be one of the biggest changes to your home life and to your career. Nursery school, while universal in Sweden, does not start until your child is one year old. If you require care before then, you will be looking at employing a private nanny which is very costly as the state system is designed to encourage parents to stay home with very young children. While pregnant, there are different kinds of sick leaves available, but you do have the right to start taking parental leave prior to the birth of your child. When your child is born, your partner will have 10 days (in Sweden) to be at home with you. These days are in essence obligatory—fathers will not win glory points at work for not taking these days and you cannot save them for later.

During the first year, both parents should expect to be at home at some level of leave. The average age children start at nursery is around 15–18 months. Application to the nursery system will vary from place to place, but you need to plan to apply well before the time you want your child to start. There are often long queues and these are managed by municipal or state authorities. Information regarding this process is updated regularly via municipal websites or your jurisdictional equivalent, and will vary from region to region, so keeping abreast of local information will be essential to your planning process.

Having access to universal nursery is very conducive to working parents, but expect some degree of uncertainty. You may not get a spot at the nursery you want or you may not hear until quite near the acceptance date. Dates are determined by the nursery, along with local government authorities. This can make the first year stressful, especially when wanting to plan research schedules. However, be patient—you will get a spot and generally the quality of childcare is high.

Some families share the later months of the first year; both parents work part-time and are on leave part-time in order to mitigate these uncertainties. These different percentages shared between parents are very common and your institution will be familiar with these solutions. Parental leave is highly protected by the state, and with open communication most solutions for work-life balance are positively treated by employers. Grandparents and other relatives can also provide stop-gaps though this is not often an option for international families. Private nurseries for children under the age of one are not legal in Sweden and will not be regulated by the state.

After the First Year

After the first year things get really complicated as a working parent! There are many ways that parental leave and supports continue beyond the newborn stage and leave policies will continue to affect your daily scheduling as well as your research plans. This requires a fundamental shift in thinking in how to plan your leave periods and work relationships. The parental leave system is geared to be used in accordance with your life course needs rather than provide a short-term solution to infant care that you may be more familiar with in other state systems.

For many PhD candidates, this means that returning to work can be done at various percentage levels—for example, in Sweden, parents have the right to apply for up to a 25% leave of absence until their children are eight years old. More commonly though, parents can take one day a week as leave or use their leave to create shorter work days. It is also important to know that saving parental days to use later (up until your child is eight in Sweden) is common—such as to take time off for Summer breaks and Fall holidays. If you have more than one child, each parent could be taking leave at different percentage levels for each child. Unlike many other workplace contexts, planning your leave can be applied to the first eight years of parenting, or up until the children start school. In the case of Sweden, days not used by the time children are eight years of age are lost. This means you must think that leave is not only for care of young children but a way to structure this turbulent period of family change and transition and career building. Taken together, the opportunities for customization are endless, so when asking working parents in Scandinavia how they balance work-life schedules, their solutions are as varied as each family is distinct.

Familiarize yourself with the different policies available at your disposal as they will impact your work very specifically. For example, VAB days (colloquial for vård av barn 'care of child') are given to care for your children when ill in Sweden; these days are paid by the state and are available to parents and other care givers. For many PhD candidates, these days are 'off the clock', so you may receive these days at the end of your PhD contract in terms of time. It is important to keep records of VAB days for discussing contract lengths, especially near the end of your PhD contract. In some instances, the accumulation of these days (and the nurseries will not tolerate sick children being sent to nursery) can add months of 'make-up' time to your work. One colleague recently had approximately 50 days added to his contract to account for VAB days. This is a huge benefit to PhD candidates but requires careful record keeping and knowledge about your plans and time lines. It is useful have an excel file of your VAB and leave days to help you keep track of all your and your partner's activities.

Your workday will be shaped by other institutions in addition to your work department duties, such as the nursery's hours and your drop-off and pick-up times. Most parents share drop-off and pick-up, and it is not unusual in workplaces for many working parents to leave at 3pm (and arrive early). It is the norm when scheduling meetings, seminars and other research activities to consider your colleagues' schedules around family life and it is perfectly fair to say, yourself, that you have these hours at the university (these may be more complicated in the private sector). Parental leave is generally very well respected and this is important in the social life of your workplace. Respecting your colleagues need to VAB, parental leave, and to participate equally in childcare is a strong social norm and not respecting these boundaries will alienate you within your department.

Research schedules throughout the PhD education period need to be timed and contextualized with your leave schedules. Issues such as field work, ongoing ethics reviews, funding timing, writing plans, access to laboratories and data sets are all important to consider in your timeline and in your family schedule as well. Important issues such as access to shared databases/timelines need to be fully discussed with your research partners. Rules and regulations may change while you are on leave, during your extensions or while you accrue time away or work lower percentage levels. For some on research grants, these rules will be challenging to navigate, and for others it will simply be a matter of applying to funding bodies for the leave which will be granted as part of the legal framework. What is important to know is that it is not unusual to plan too far in advance—even a year or two ahead—to accommodate different researchers' needs. This is particularly important if you are working in a research team or project where other people's leave time will also be part of the project planning.

It is important to speak with your supervisor and project managers to negotiate scheduling with a long-term view in mind, not just your initial time away with a newborn. It is also possible that your supervisor is not familiar with all the current rules and your rights due to the complexity of the policies. If in doubt, contact your department heads, ombudsman, and even your union. Joining your field's union is important for support and for getting unemployment insurance for after your PhD candidacy. The official information sources, in Sweden *Försakringskassen*, will have information readily available. Going to the official sources is ideal for getting the most recent information or to understand how different policies align.

Making Flexibility Work for You

Once you know the options, it is useful to think about doing different kind of tasks at different stages of your PhD education. For example, as I lowered my work percentage I sometimes took a semester off from teaching in order to focus on writing and research. You earn time in lieu for your leave so a year of parental leave will add one year to a contract. These add-ons can be easily calculated for your initial leaves after your baby is born, however, as your child grows and you take different percentages or periods off it can be difficult to calculate your new time scales. It is not unusual to ask for time to consider your options and to say you need to discuss with your partner and their work place schedules.

Other practicalities to consider are how to balance intensive work periods, such as field work or laboratory studies. It could be during these periods you reduce the percentage of leave and work 100%, balancing out with your partner that they take a higher percentage of leave. For many PhD candidates, labour intensive periods can be complemented by your partner taking leave, even with older children. My own partner would occasionally work only 80% while I was in a busy period, freeing me to work longer days. Partners can also take parental leave to follow you into the field. The responsibility of leave-taking should be considered at the household scale—fostering gender equality—and not only by individuals providing care.

For hectic periods, such as your last year of study, it is possible to change the hours at your child's nursery, but it is usual to give a month's notice on significant changes. It is also not reasonable to assume that a nursery place will be maintained for you because you are paying for a spot, if away for field work. Most municipalities will not keep unused spots and will give those spots to other families in the queue. In Stockholm, a child can only be removed from nursery with a guaranteed return spot for 3 months. You will get a spot upon your return but usually through re-entering the queue system. Again, a myriad of solutions are possible; it is just a matter of finding out what you are entitled to get, how far in advance changes need to be made and understanding that you will be negotiating these practicalities with the state, not a private nursery.

Final Words of Advice

Think of your parental leave as a structure that will shape the course of your PhD studies. You are not just planning for a short period while you have an infant, but for the entire PhD project as a working parent/family. Ask how leave needs to be fitted into your research schedule. Keep the lines of communication open and don't be afraid to talk about your planned leaves and how you are going to make it work with your senior researchers.

Becoming a parent in Scandinavia will sometimes be a combination of short-term child care solutions, but more often than not, it will require a lot of thinking and planning about the myriad of policies at your disposal. Three central takeaways to consider are that you don't know what you don't know; you have to remember that child leave is not just for new babies; and that there are probably very few places that offer so many options for finding a work-life balance, so work it smart. Find a way that works best for you, your child and your career, by being strategic.

References

Caretta, M. A., & Webster, N. A. (2016). "What kept me going was stubbornness": Perspectives from Swedish early career women academics in geography. *Investigaciones Feministas, 7*(2), 89–113.

Drozdzewski, D., & Robinson, D. F. (2015). Care-work on fieldwork: Taking your own children into the field. *Children's Geographies, 13*(3), 372–378.

Gill, R., & Donaghue, N. (2016). Resilience, apps and reluctant individualism: Technologies of self in the neoliberal academy. *Women's Studies International Forum, 54,* 91–99.

Hawkins, R., Manzi, M., & Ojeda, D. (2014). Lives in the making: Power, academia and the everyday. *ACME: An International E-Journal for Critical Geographies, 13*(2), 328–351.

Klocker, N., & Drozdzewski, D. (2012). Commentary. *Environment and Planning A, 44*(6), 1271–1277.

CHAPTER FIFTEEN

Boundary Spanning Research

The Industrial PhD

CARSTEN LUND PEDERSEN

Introduction

There is a unique PhD program in Denmark which is entitled 'the Industrial PhD program'.[1] The program is unique in the sense that the student is employed by a host organization or company to conduct a research project—while simultaneously being enrolled as a doctoral student at a university. The industrial PhD student must not only conduct research while he or she is embedded within the organization, obtain academic PhD training at the university and live up to the same formal requirements as traditional PhD students—they must also manage the diverse interests of both the host organization and the university.

For an industrial PhD student, this setup can be both immensely rewarding as well as challenging. It is rewarding as you will have the chance to immerse yourself in an organization throughout the entire project period, with a chance to gain unique access to data. It is likely that your research results will subsequently be applied in 'the real world' and not 'only' disseminated in research papers. However, it can be challenging as you are required to span the boundaries between the host organization and the academic world, where you will need to deal with conflicting interests between these domains, as well as internal organizational politics. These issues can be overwhelming, as the necessary experience in dealing with industrial PhDs at universities or host organizations is typically lacking (Nielsen, 2014,

2015). This, in turn, means that students often do not obtain sufficient guidance on these issues in the process. The methodological literature on action research provides useful insight on academia-practice collaborations (Coghlan & Brannick, 2014; Evered & Louis, 1981; Schultz & Hatch, 2005; Van de Ven, 2007), but they fail to explain the challenges encountered in industrial PhD projects. This chapter addresses that shortcoming. Industrial PhDs are engaged in three different domains: Academia, practice, and the interaction between the two. The industrial PhD student is thus *boundary spanning*. The main differences and similarities between the three domains that an industrial PhD must span are covered in this chapter, and concrete advice for prospective students is provided.

What is an Industrial PhD?

The industrial PhD program is a research setup that is unique to Denmark. As most other PhD programs, the expected duration of the project is three years. Unlike other PhD programs, the industrial PhD requires that the project is industrially focused, that the student is employed by a host company, and enrolled at a university at the same time (The Industrial PhD Programme, 2017). An industrial PhD project thus inherently has a dual focus: you must fulfill the same academic requirements as other PhD students *and* be industrially focused.

In Denmark, the industrial PhD program is managed by Innovation Fund Denmark, while The Industrial PhD & PostDoc Association seeks to advance the interests and preserve the reputation of its members (Erhvervsphdforeningen, 2017). While this chapter is based on a Danish experience, many of the issues that will be touched upon are similarly relevant for other academia-practice collaborations

Conducting Boundary Spanning Research

In an industrial PhD project you will need to span both academic and organizational boundaries, while seeking to make the two interact. Being a 'boundary spanner' implies that you continuously transition between the academic and practice-based worlds. The interaction between academia and practice is a type of 'grey zone', where you, as an industrial PhD student, will need to balance the interests of the two different worlds. This interaction may be tangible, in the form of meetings between the organization and your university supervisors, but it is most often intangible in the form of issues and questions which you need to grapple with along the way. This grey zone *is* the boundary spanning area for the industrial PhD student. Table 15.1 compares the differences and similarities between the three domains. The table is based on my own experience as an industrial PhD student and the relevant theoretical guidance I have been able to find during the process.

Table 15.1: Comparing the three domains of an industrial PhD project.

	Academia	Boundary spanning	Practice
Interest in the project	What is true?	How to combine?	What works?
Emphasis	Rigor	Best of both worlds	Relevance
Possible time horizon	Long-term, several years	Long-term, short-term	Short-term, few months
Role of researcher	Detached onlooker	Boundary spanner	Active participant
Type of learning	Learning-by-reflecting	Reflecting while doing	Learning-by-doing
Type of knowledge created	Explicit knowledge	Meta-knowledge	Experiential knowledge
Value in relation to project	Distance to the empirical phenomenon	Academically and practically relevant	Unique access in terms of data and the field
Desired output	New findings, publications	Synergy, happy partners	Relevant advice, business improvement
Potential issues	Academic requirements	Balancing interests	Organizational politics

Source: Author.

The academic domain is preoccupied with *what is true*, novelty of your results and contributions of your work, and how valid and reliable your findings are. On the other hand, the organization is interested in *what works*, that your research works in practice and that it is relevant for the organization. The boundary spanning domain is preoccupied with *how to combine* the different interests of the academic and practice domains. How can we gain value from the interaction of results that convey *what is true* and *what works in practice?* An industrial PhD student has to address the 'double hurdle' of obtaining academic quality and practical relevance (Pettigrew, 2001). Academia emphasizes rigor, practice emphasizes practical relevance, and the boundary spanning domain seeks to obtain the best of both worlds. How can we obtain both academic rigor and practical relevance?

Another important aspect is the differing time horizons conventionally adopted in the different domains. An academic perspective often adopts a time horizon of several years, as both the PhD duration and publication process tend to be quite long. The practice domain can sometimes have a time horizon of a few months, as employees often need to deliver results every quarter (depending on the organization). As a result, the boundary spanning domain between the two worlds can sometimes be challenging, as you will need to balance both the long-term aspect of doing research with a potential short-term focus on updating relevant employees from practice about the research.

The role of the researcher and the type of learning and knowledge that is created is another boundary presenting challenges. In many academic domains, you are expected to be a detached onlooker who learns by reflecting, and who creates explicit knowledge that can be disseminated and further assessed and tested. The practice domain, on the other hand, sees you as an active participant in the organization, where you learn by doing and accumulate experiential knowledge. Your role as a boundary spanner is that of reflecting while you are doing, and building up meta-knowledge, that is, knowledge about different types of knowledge. This means that you know which types of learning/knowledge are needed within an academic setting, which types of learning/knowledge are created within a practice setting, and especially how the two can be combined. There are different forms of reflection: the issues at hand, the process, and the underlying assumptions (Mezirow, 1991).

As your project ultimately ends up being assessed by a committee of experts, it is essential to understand the expected output and potential issues that each of the three domains have. The academic domain expects you to produce unique, relevant, and rigorous findings that will be part of your final dissertation. The practice domain expects relevant and practical advice that can help them improve their business. It may also be expected that you help with an intervention within the organization. Your research may even be used in a new product, technology or process within the organization. The ideal output is synergy between academia and practice as well as satisfied project partners.

Practical Advice for When You Begin

Have a diverse network in all three domains: No student will ever be able to understand all of the relevant domain knowledge and complexities by themselves. It could take a lifetime to fully understand either the ways of an academic career or the constantly evolving dynamics of a large organization. Make sure you have a diverse network of mentors to guide you on the academic path, and practitioners from the organization that can guide you within the organizational boundaries, as well as other industrial PhD students. In combination, such a network can make up a personal advisory board. In my own project, I benefitted from my supervisors (both my academic and my company supervisors), as the academic supervisors were able to provide the needed academic counseling, whereas the company supervisor could ask the right questions in terms of the practical relevance of the research.

Learn to communicate to different types of audiences: The industrial PhD program necessitates dissemination to both academics and practitioners. As these audiences follow different norms, expectations, and interests in communication, you need to be able to communicate to both audiences, and to translate between the two worlds. Giving presentations is important in both academia and industry, and the most important thing is to structure them so that the messages are clear. Draw upon your network of people from both domains to help you develop and perfect this skill. In my own project, I would often let my academic colleagues review my presentations before academic seminars or conferences (to make sure that they were suitable for an academic audience). I also let my colleagues from the organization look through my slides if I had an important presentation there (to make sure that it would not be too academic). As part of the PhD, I also refined this skill at events arranged by my university, where the task was to 'pitch our PhDs' to practitioners.

Time management is your new best friend: You need to divide your time between your organization and university. This requires you to be skilled in time management, as industrial PhD projects can be immensely time-consuming. This skill is helpful when you need to shift between long-term time horizons (academia) and short-term time horizons (practice), with an eye for both. In my own project, I benefitted from having a plan and *Gantt chart*[2] for each semester and year, in addition to each day formulating my 2–3 Most Important Tasks (my MITs) for the day (Kaufman, 2012).

Industrial PhD research projects can be emotionally demanding: The boundary spanning role discussed earlier puts you under emotional pressure with many ups and downs. Although the demands of boundary spanning research cannot be changed, actively anticipate and prepare for it by talking to colleagues, supervisors and friends in your network throughout the process. Keep a research diary to record your thoughts and feelings, and use it as a source for reflections during the project (Van Maanen, 1988).

Have problem-swapping partners: Find problem-swapping partners, people in your network from whom you can obtain a different perspective on a problem you are facing. These partners can be other industrial PhD students working in a different industry. Not only does this provide you additional support for problem solving, it is also a source of diverse streams of insight. Thinking differently has been shown to be related to better problem-solving and a way to circumvent your own blind spots (Page, 2007).

Look for anomalies in the collaboration: The academic and practice domains have different interests in your project. Exploit this opportunity to conduct unique research by actively looking for anomalies where what is 'true' does not work, or what is not 'true' actually seems to work in practice. When you encounter such anomalies, make a theoretical contribution based on your empirical observations. In this way, you conduct interesting research that provides new knowledge of both academic and practical value. Many paradigm-shifting studies have been inspired by observation of anomalies. Also, shifting the focus from building practice from theory to building theory from practice can in itself be rewarding and valuable (Schultz & Hatch, 2005).

Do not conduct the research on your own: It is beneficial to not conduct the research on your own, without the active involvement of supervisors and relevant people in your network. The project needs a collective effort to succeed. Collaborate with different people in order to balance the challenging circumstances of boundary spanning work in industrial PhD projects.

Remember that the industrial PhD is a research project: At the end of the day, the academic requirements are ultimately most important. When facing conflicting interests, remember that academic requirements must take precedence over practice-based needs. Maintain your non-negotiable requirement to be able to conduct independent research.

Remember to listen to yourself: Do not, in an attempt to please your project partners, forget yourself in the process. You conduct the research because of your personal ambition and curiosity. This is crucial to remember to maintain the motivation to complete the project.

Conclusion

An industrial PhD project holds the potential of producing valuable, interesting and challenging research. The combination of academic and practical interests tends to spur deeper modes of learning (Argyris, 1976). However, as a prospective industrial PhD student be aware of and acknowledge the need to span different domains. This can lead to a variety of issues. Be aware of the different expectations and realities, and make sure to have a diverse network of people who can support you and possibly act as problem-swapping partners. An industrial PhD is first and foremost a research project, so the academic requirements should be the first priority. Focus on yourself in the process. Often the conflicting stakes, interests and domains can crowd out your own inner voice as a researcher—which should not be the case. The research project may span boundaries and include different partners, but it is driven by your own curiosity and intrinsic motivation. Do not forget yourself and your own interests during your industrial PhD project.

Notes

1. To the best of my knowledge, there is not a directly comparable PhD program to the Danish model in the other Scandinavian countries. However, while the program is unique, it can still be related to other academia-practice research collaborations.
2. A Gantt chart is a type of bar chart that illustrates different activities in a project schedule. It is often used in project management. Additional information and templates for Gantt charts are widely available on the internet.

References

Argyris, C. (1976). Single-loop and double-loop models in research on decision making. *Administrative Science Quarterly, 21*(3), 363–375.

Coghlan, D., & Brannick, T. (2014). *Doing action research in your own organization*. Thousand Oaks, CA: Sage Publications.

Erhvervsphdforeningen. (2017). *About us*. Retrieved from http://www.erhvervsphdforeningen.dk/

Evered, R., & Louis, M. (1981). Alternative perspectives in the organizational sciences: "Inquiry from the inside" and "inquiry from the outside". *The Academy of Management Review, 6*(3), 385–395.

Kaufman, J. (2012). *The personal MBA: Master the art of business*. New York, NY: Penguin.

Mezirow, J. (1991). *Transformative dimensions of adult learning*. San Francisco, CA: Jossey-Bass.

Nielsen, R. K. (2014). *Global mindset as managerial meta-competence and organizational capability: Boundary-crossing leadership cooperation in the MN. The case of 'group mindset' in Solar A/S.* Frederiksberg: Copenhagen Business School (PhD).

Nielsen, R. K. (2015). *Kommentar: Er du klar til erhvervs-PhD funding?* Retrieved from http://medie.cbs.dk/kommentar-er-du-klar-til-erhvervs-phd-funding

Page, S. (2007). *The difference: How the power of diversity creates better groups, firms, schools and societies*. Princeton, NJ: Princeton University Press.

Pettigrew, A. M. (2001). Management research after modernism. *British Journal of Management, 12*, 61–70.

Schultz, M., & Hatch, M. J. (2005). Building theory from practice. *Strategic Organization, 3*(3), 337–348.

The Industrial PhD Programme. (2017). *The industrial PhD programme*. Retrieved from http://ufm.dk/en/research-and-innovation/funding-programmes-for-research-and-innovation/find-danish-funding-programmes/programmes-managed-by-innovation-fund-denmark/industrial-phd

Van de Ven, A. H. (2007). *Engaged scholarship—A guide for organizational and social research*. Oxford: Oxford University Press.

Van Maanen, J. (1988). *Tales of the field: On writing ethnography*. Chicago, IL: University of Chicago Press.

PART FIVE

Going North to Study

CHAPTER SIXTEEN

No Tuition at All?

Opportunities for the International Student

JULIE A. NIZIURSKI, JUDY BRUCE, SHARON STEIN, AND CHRISTOPHER McMASTER

Introduction

When I (Chris) first heard that doctoral study in Nordic countries (including Finland and Iceland) was tuition-free, I was suitably impressed. As the Scandinavians have a reputation for social awareness and welfare, including education, I wasn't surprised. But when I heard that tuition-free doctoral study also included international students, I definitely wanted to learn more.

Cost is a very real inhibitor to postgraduate study. *The Atlantic* refers to debt as the 'dirty little secret' of doctoral programs in the United States. Estimates are that, when finishing with the coveted doctoral degree, students will have on average a hefty $30,000 debt (Weissmann, 2014). More often than not, that debt is compounded with already existing student loans. The *Financial Times* reports that students in the UK leave university with even more debt than their American counterparts (Vi□a, 2016). Budget changes in Australia could mean that a doctoral degree there will cost up to $30,000 (Bexley, 2014). It is a similar story throughout the English-speaking world.

The bottom line is that a PhD can cost a good deal of money. Not only is cost a potential factor in dissuading enrolment in a doctoral program, it can also play a part in the high attrition rate seen in doctoral programmes.

It is an enticing formula: Doctoral study in Scandinavia is tuition-free, and most doctoral study in Scandinavia is conducted in the English language (which is why this edition of the *Survive and Succeed* series is in English). Doctoral programmes in Scandinavian institutions accept international students. So why don't more English speaking international students flock to a Scandinavian university to study? One answer could be that they do not even know the opportunity exists.

In this chapter, we will explore these opportunities. As editor, I have invited three 'international' students to share their experiences. Each studied (or is still studying) in Scandinavia. The primary purpose of this chapter is to highlight the potential to study in Scandinavia for students residing in other countries.

Judy completed her PhD through the University of Oulu in Finland while living in New Zealand where she worked as a lecturer in teacher education at the University of Canterbury. Julie is from the United States and is currently completing her PhD in psychology at Aarhus University, Denmark. She had never been to Europe before moving to Denmark. Sharon is a doctoral student from the USA, currently studying in Canada. She went to Finland for three months as a visiting doctoral researcher on a large international project funded by the Finnish Academy.

This chapter is structured as a conversation, as if Julie, Sharon and Judy are sitting around a table at a coffee house fielding questions from an inquisitive prospective student. As the table is large enough, you are invited to join us.

No Tuition Fees? For Real? Did You Find Any Hidden Costs?

Julie: No cost at all. This is huge since I already owe the USA government a ridiculous amount of money for the cost of my undergraduate and Master's education. I would not have been able to afford to get my PhD if I had stayed in the USA.

Judy: While I didn't pay fees, I was required to fund most of my own travel, and also accommodation and living costs while in Oulu. My situation was unusual in that I was employed full time as a lecturer at another university. Because my employer supported my research work, I did receive a study grant for my second visit to Oulu.

Sharon: That wasn't really applicable for me, since I was officially working as an employee and not a student. My salary was paid through the project I was working on, which covered most of the costs of my three-month stay. In this, I was unusually fortunate, but opportunities for international graduate experiences do exist, and I would encourage students who are interested in such experiences to pursue them, and also encourage supervisors to help create possibilities like this for their students.

While study is tuition-free for students from the European Union, fees for non-EU students have recently been introduced in Sweden and Denmark. In those two countries, self-financing international students can be eligible for scholarships and financial aid (see links at the end of the chapter for detailed advice). In Finland and Denmark, there are no tuition fees on Doctoral level study, regardless of your nationality.

How Did You Locate a University and Supervisor?

Judy: Prior to embarking on my PhD in Finland, I was working in teacher education. My focus in this role was teaching and research in the area of social justice education. During that time, I began working with a colleague on a large research project investigating shifts in the conceptualisation of knowledge and learning. I was challenged and inspired to be a part of this project as I began to engage in critical global citizenship education to make sense of contemporary changes in education. The colleague I was working with invited me to extend this research work and embark on my PhD. Around this time, she was appointed as professor of Global Education at the University of Oulu, Finland. I was consequently able to enrol at the same university and take part in the PhD program there.

During most of my PhD studies I only had one supervisor. It wasn't until the final stages of my PhD that I engaged a second supervisor. This was suggested by my first supervisor. While it may be considered unusual to have just one supervisor, it was advantageous in my situation as I was also working with a team of experienced researchers at my own university where I was employed in a teaching and research role. I already had research and writing experience prior to engaging in my PhD, and I wanted to work quickly and independently. Additionally, I had an excellent professional relationship with my supervisor, and I was aware that there were risks in engaging another supervisor, particularly as there wasn't anyone else at the time at the University of Oulu who shared the same theoretical perspective that I was using in my study. The second supervisor who came on board later in my study was recently employed at the University of Oulu and was actively researching in a similar field. This was a good decision, as she brought fresh eyes to my writing and helped with the final critical stages of my study.

Julie: My Master's thesis advisors in the USA had visited Aarhus University, and when discussing my future they suggested it could be a great fit for me. I contacted my current supervisor and she first offered me a 6-month position in order to see if I liked it in Denmark, which I did, so I then applied to the PhD program.

While at Texas, my main thesis advisors came and visited the center which I am now affiliated with at Aarhus University. When they returned, I was about to hand in my Master's thesis, so I was discussing with them my future options. One of them suggested I contact the leader of the center in Denmark. I applied to the PhD program and my application was given to the center leader, who then offered me a job. After being in Denmark for a few months, I reapplied to the PhD program and was accepted. I now have about a year left in my PhD, but hope to find a job in Denmark after I am done.

I also contacted a professor in Australia and was in talks with a potential position there when I got the offer in Denmark. Just contact people if you find their work to be of interest. Be sure to show a knowledge of the kind of work they do and explain why you think that working with them will benefit yourself as well as them. You definitely need to sell yourself. Also, take advantage of modern technology; offer to skype with them as putting a face to the name is always nice. Don't be frustrated if you apply to a program and don't get accepted right away. Understand that you may come from a different educational culture which looks for different criteria in an application. Once I got to Denmark with the job offer, I reapplied to the PhD program with the new knowledge, and with help from my advisor it made a strong application.

Sharon: I was a doctoral student from the USA, studying in Canada, and went to Finland for three months as visiting doctoral researcher on a large international project funded by the Finnish Academy. I was located at the University of Oulu, where my boss/dissertation committee member had previously worked and secured the grant. Because she is located in Canada now, I did not have a supervisor while in Oulu, but worked closely with (and relied heavily) on one of her PhD students who was also working on the project.

How Often Did You Have to, or Did You, Go to Your Scandinavian Institution?

As Julie has chosen to live and study here, and Sharon only studied for a limited time, I'll ask Judy this question.

Judy: I travelled from New Zealand to Finland three times during my time of study. Initially, I participated in some course work, which was a requirement of the PhD programme. My second visit was for a longer three-month stay where I focussed on reading, and writing for publication (also a requirement). My final visit was for my defence. As I only travelled to Finland on three occasions, most of my supervisor contact was via Skype and e-mail. This worked well for me as my supervisor always responded promptly online to any queries, and she gave detailed written feedback frequently. For complex research conversations, we used Skype and this also worked very well. I was also able to connect with other postgraduate students there through a series of online lectures. I was able to listen to the lectures live, and ask questions in live time. This was another excellent platform for staying connected with the research community there, as well as others who were linked from different countries around the world. Today, there are multiple online platforms available to assist with interconnectivity globally, and we took full advantage of this for the purposes of completing my PhD.

Do You Think There Were Any Advantages from Studying Domestically, and What Were They?

Judy: To me there were many advantages to being able to study at a university in Finland. One of these was the opportunity to engage with the Global Education programme at Oulu University, including the chance to connect with an international community of scholars. That is something I would not have had were I to study through a domestic institution.

The other advantage, even though I was half a world away, was that I felt very supported. The university was well organised and offered an in-depth doctoral programme. As an 'outsider' there was some assumed institutional knowledge that I missed. Some administrative procedures weren't clearly explained, or else I had to work quite hard to find the right channels of information. These were relatively minor issues, however, and there was a very supportive group of other PhD students who helped me directly. The university did provide small grants for presentations at international conferences, and small grants for travel within Europe.

How Is Your Degree Acknowledged or Recognised in Your Home Country?

Julie: Aarhus University is an accredited university, so my PhD will be recognized as any other PhD. In my personal opinion, I think I also get the added bonus of having the experience of studying abroad and learning from people of different cultures, which I would not have been able to do as extensively in the USA.

Judy: The University of Oulu is a reputable university. My field of study is education, and the Finnish education system has a significant global reputation. Additionally, there are many similarities between New Zealand and Finland. Consequently, my PhD was recognised and respected in my home country.

picked up from the airport, and showed me around the town. I am forever indebted to him. We are now writing a chapter together comparing the internationalization processes of universities in Canada and Finland!

What Should I Absolutely Know Before I Do This? What Are the Tricks or Traps? Any Parting Words?

Judy: Finding the right supervisor is absolutely critical to any PhD study. I delayed enrolling until I found someone I knew would challenge and extend me in ways that I needed. I had a good connection both professionally and personally, and so I was pretty certain it was going to work well. This made studying by distance possible and even enjoyable. It helped that I had a good group of researchers in my own university that I could sound out ideas with.

Another thing that would help is finding someone who has good institutional knowledge where you will be studying, ideally, another PhD student with more experience than you. Sometimes admin systems and processes can be confusing. A friendly fellow student can work as a 'translator' in these situations. Surround yourself with good support.

You need to consider your resources, personal and financial. Any PhD is stressful, so minimising stress in other areas of your life is critical to an emotionally more stable journey. If you can ensure, as much as possible, that you are not going to have to stress about finances, then that will help a great deal.

Maybe what stands out is the willingness to be adaptable throughout the process, to step out with courage into the unknown, and to seek out support both professionally and personally. I think it is a journey that requires a level of determination and focus. PhD study is difficult enough, while being in your own cultural context, but studying elsewhere presents professional and personal challenges as students are living in a foreign cultural context. There are advantages to studying in the Scandinavian context, such as no fees, minimal costs, and English language medium, but it is also necessary to be mindful of the challenges, and consider ways of preparing a little for what might come your way on this journey.

Julie: Be prepared to feel lonely. The winters are hard. I learned my first winter here, that 'Winter is Coming' is not just a quote from *Game of Thrones*, it is a real threat in Denmark. The Danes are extremely nice and if you ask for help, they will help you in any way that they can. However, they have their own lives and established relationships, and it can be hard to get connected outside of work. I highly recommend, if you are single, a dating app. This helped me get out of my apartment and meet people.

Finding housing in Denmark is difficult and extremely expensive. Be prepared to pay three months' deposit plus three months' rent up front. You have to check all the housing websites constantly and reply to as many postings as possible. It is easier to find a place once you are in Aarhus, as many places have open houses where they invite potential tenants to see the place, which is hard to attend if you are not in the country. I had the most luck with BoligPortal.dk (see more links at the end of the chapter).

If you are coming from the USA, it is a long trip home, so immerse yourself in the Danish way of life. Adapt to your new surroundings. The summers are fantastic. It is easy to travel to see the rest of Europe. Yes, it will be lonely at times, but do everything you can to get out of your apartment and interact with the Danes. Joining the local gym helped, as did going to any event a Dane may happen to invite me to, and joining the local International Club.

Sharon: It was fascinating and refreshing to be in the Finnish university context, where students are not (or at least not yet) conceived of as customers in the same way they are in the USA. Even the fact that meals on campus are highly subsidized was a marvel to me, as there is no 'discount' at USA universities, and housing and dining are in many cases important sources of revenue for institutions. It was an important reminder that higher education can be organized differently, however unlikely that may appear. At the same time, I felt great anxiety about what might happen in the Finnish context if it starts moving toward a more business-like model of higher education, as has already happened in many anglophone countries. The recent move toward charging tuition for non-EU international students not only limits accessibility, but it may introduce further business logics that will then permeate the rest of the institution. Finland and other places need to think long and hard about what may be lost once they go down this road, and perhaps learn from the mistakes made in places like the USA, Australia, and the UK, who have thoroughly privatized and marketized their higher education systems.

Nothing is ever 'free', including doctoral study in Scandinavia. Even for those for whom there are no tuition fees, there are other costs involved, both direct and indirect. Not just the cost of room, board, and books, but also the different challenges of negotiating one's place as a visitor in a foreign country and one's absence from home. These costs and challenges may look very different depending on one's positionalities. I think it is important to highlight the possibilities for study in Scandinavia, but as with anywhere, it is important not to romanticise, either, or to generalize the experience for everyone.

Judy, Sharon and Julie illustrate how doable it is to take advantage of the opportunity study in Scandinavia presents. Below are links to portals that will allow you to continue the discussion started in this chapter.

References

PhD programs have a dirty secret: Student debt. (2014, July 14). *The Atlantic.* Retrieved from https://www.theatlantic.com/business/archive/2014/01/phd-programs-have-a-dirty-secret-student-debt/283126/

Raising the cost of a PhD. (2014, May 14). *The Conversation.* Retrieved from http://theconversation.com/raising-the-cost-of-a-phd-26912

UK graduates leave university with more debt than US peers. (2016, April 27). *Financial Times.* Retrieved from https://www.ft.com/content/a1c27f38-0c86-11e6-b0f1-61f222853ff3

Links for studying in Scandinavia

Study in Sweden: https://studyinsweden.se

Studyinsweden.se is a comprehensive, official resource on studying in Sweden for prospective and current international students. Here you'll find everything you need to know on the Swedish higher education system, finding and applying for a programme, searching for scholarships, living as an international student in Sweden and learning Swedish. You can also explore Sweden's many universities and hear from accomplished alumni on how choosing Sweden changed their lives.

Study in Denmark: http://studyindenmark.dk

Danish PhD scholarships are fully funded, i.e. you receive a salary and there is no tuition fee. Some PhD programmes are developed as partnerships between universities and private companies.

This portal offers links to individual universities in Denmark.

Study in Finland: http://www.studyinfinland.fi/home

Official site offering all you need to know to get started to study in Finland.

Study in Norway: http://www.studyinnorway.no/

The official gateway to Norwegian education. Find your study programme and explore study possibilities in Norway.

Study in Iceland: http://www.studyiniceland.is/id/1447

This site provides information on all higher education institutions in Iceland, as well as practical things to know and do before arriving.

Top Universities: https://www.topuniversities.com/student-info/choosing-university/why-study-scandinavian-university

If you're planning to study in Europe, then **Scandinavian universities** should definitely be on your list. Find out why you should consider studying in Denmark, Sweden or Norway—or nearby Finland or Iceland (these last two are not technically part of Scandinavia, but are within the Nordic group).

Top universities offer a good overview of the benefits and provides links to each country.

PhD Portal: http://www.phdportal.com/

Offers links to PhD programs in other countries. Simply type in a Nordic country into the search bar and explore. Useful information regarding visas, money, travel, etc.

BoligPortal: http://www.boligportal.dk/en/

Useful portal for finding accommodation.

Scholarship for Development: http://www.scholars4dev.com/4031/list-of-european-countries-with-tuition-freelow-tuition-universities-colleges/

If you fail to qualify for fully-funded university scholarships, consider enrolling in universities that are tuition-free or charge low tuition fees or those offering tuition fee waivers. Countries like Norway, Austria, Germany, Finland, and Sweden offer different types of free/low tuition schemes and tuition waivers for international students. scholars4dev.com has compiled information and provided links to tuition-free Colleges and Universities and links to Universities offering tuition scholarships.

post-doctoral positions or funding. Even if you're already qualified for a position, speaking Scandinavian also signals your commitment to the local milieu, (hopefully) improving your chances of getting hired within Scandinavia. Your demonstrable willingness to integrate and engage with local culture will similarly benefit you elsewhere.

There are also non-academic dividends to learning the local language. While it is perfectly possible to lead an active social life in Scandinavia without speaking the local language, the tough process of finding friends and establishing yourself socially—already tougher than in much of the world due to the reserved nature of Scandinavian culture—will be slowed by not learning some of the language. As such, you can generally build up your 'social capital' with even relatively minor investments (Field, 2003). This, recent research suggests, can in turn improve your language acquisition (Smith, Giraud-Carrier, Dewey, Ring, & Gore, 2011). Whether your reasons are principled or pragmatic, there are lots of reasons to speak Scandinavian.

How to Learn

Once you've decided to learn the local language the next decision is how you're going to do so. A key point here is that *there is no one way to learn a language.* Just as people learn languages for different purposes, so too there are many, many tools and methods available to the modern learner, from books and traditional classrooms to online courses and apps. Find whatever method (or combination of methods) works for you. Unless you have extensive language-learning experience, this will likely be a trial-and-error process. It's worth planning with the knowledge that the lifestyle of most PhD students, especially those moving to a new country, can be erratic, making regular dedicated study-time a luxury.

Regardless of the tools you decide to employ, your attitude to learning Scandinavian should be 'slow and steady wins the race'. Don't try to become conversational in a single semester. It's not impossible, but doing so would leave little time for your day job, let alone anything else in your life. Try setting milestone goals for yourself as a way of both tracking your progress, and of mitigating the frustration of moving more slowly than you might like to. Your goal for one semester may be to be able to have a basic conversation with a colleague over coffee; while a later milestone might be to attend (and understand) a lecture in Scandinavian. You might aim to become conversational, or even fluent, over the course of your PhD, and work towards that alongside your studies. Good final milestones might be giving a conference paper of your own, or even publishing a short text before the end of your studies.

Such steady work obviously requires a good deal of perseverance, but it should also *leave room for adaptability*. For some people, this will mean finding a set rhythm of classes and study, and sticking to it, come what may. Others may find it easier to work intensely for a while, and then cut back at busier times. Allow yourself to take breaks if you need to. Most of the people you'll encounter at the university understand the pressures on PhD students, and taking a hiatus in your language learning to concentrate on getting a chapter drafted or completing a taught course can be the difference between burning yourself out on learning Scandinavian and sticking with it for the long haul. Making learning enjoyable makes it easier to keep at, so don't be afraid to shop around for interesting books or fun classes. One way is to find an app or podcast that you enjoy, and use it during your commute, or when you exercise—little and often is better than a once-a-week marathon.

Similarly, *start small*: don't aim to explain the details of your research in Scandinavian anytime during the first few semesters of your PhD. Aim for everyday conversations with colleagues over coffee or lunch. These will give opportunities to discuss simple topics you'll probably cover early on in language classes, such as food, the weather, or hobbies. You can also use these contexts to demonstrate your progress to colleagues, and to sound out who amongst them is a kind listener, the sort of person who can modulate their language to your level and help you express yourself.

Of course, PhD students are academics, and most academics *learn by reading*. Use that strength. Pick up a newspaper on the bus, or buy a novel in Scandinavian. Assuming you're learning with the eventual goal of discussing your research with colleagues, find out what texts are set for first-semester undergraduates in your department and read them. You'll know the material, and will be able to pick up a concentrated dose of important vocabulary. You can then move on to short journal articles like conference reports or book reviews, which are particularly good if you were at the conference or have already read the book.

That said, don't neglect the oral component of language. Use apps or podcasts to expose yourself to spoken language at your own pace. TV programmes and films are also great, but try not to become over-dependant on subtitles—conferences don't provide them. Research in second-language acquisition also suggests that hobbies with social settings are great at boosting language learning (Isabellí-Garcia, 2006), and will also expose you to more everyday language than you might hear at the university. Don't worry about not learning the wrong sort of Scandinavian—not only are the Scandinavian languages characterised by small differences in register (Haugen, 1976), learning context does not appear to play a significant role in the overall success of language learning (Collentine & Freed, 2004). Joining a club or volunteering will also widen your social circle, giving you more people to practice with, and help get you out of the office or lab and integrate into your new community. Few Scandinavian academics work the long hours more common elsewhere, and Scandinavian culture is much less work-based than many others around the world.

When and Where Should You Speak Scandinavian?

Now that you're learning Scandinavian, it's time to consider when and where to speak it and when you're better off sticking to English. Most language-learning advice suggests that a learner should take every opportunity to speak their new language, but PhD students have needs beyond just language acquisition, so it's worth thinking things through carefully.

The most important thing to consider here is the context you're communicating in. Just how precisely does your audience need to understand you? Weigh the potential gain of both linguistic experience and social capital against the risks of being misunderstood, or not being able to express yourself clearly. This requires some calculating, and can feel artificial at first, but it will become second nature with time. Don't be afraid to hesitate before speaking to work out what you want to say, which language would be better, and how to express yourself. Few people hold someone thinking before answering against them, particularly in academia.

Some of the different contexts you might want to consider ahead of time can include meetings, seminars, supervisions, and even e-mails. There is nothing wrong with deciding before you even walk through the door that today is an 'English' day. Think about the formality of the setting. If you're meeting a colleague for coffee, or your supervisor for a meeting, that should be a relaxed, low-risk opportunity to strut your Scandinavian stuff. Scandinavian societies are more egalitarian than many other cultures, so even relatively formal one-on-one settings like meeting a Department Head or Dean will be just another meeting with someone who will give you their full attention and engagement, without fear of your grammar being judged.

Informal group settings like coffee breaks and lunches can be a bit tougher in some ways—a mix of voices and accents, multiple simultaneous conversations—but in other ways they are easier, allowing you to sit back and let the conversation move around you, with only the occasional comment needed on your part to signal you're still involved. Formal group settings like seminars can be even easier than informal ones. There's a built-in excuse to take a break from contributing (one speaker at a time), and the chair will often work out a list of who's speaking next. Take this time to work out what you want to say, and then start preparing your opening salvo. Listen to what the others are saying, and don't be afraid to repeat terms, or even whole phrases. Not only will it be correct, it will demonstrate you're an engaged listener. This sort of setting is usually medium-risk, but can have the highest rewards of all.

Writing e-mails is a somewhat different process, but the same considerations apply. Is it a formal or informal conversation? Are you writing to one person, or participating in a group chain? Informal correspondence is a great way to work on your written Scandinavian without fear of embarrassing yourself—if you're unclear, the person you're writing to can ask for clarification. Even more official one-on-one exchanges (with an unknown colleague in a different department, for example) are comparatively relaxed affairs in most parts of Scandinavian academic culture. Group e-mails can be a bit tougher, as it's harder for people to ask you directly if they can't puzzle out your meaning. Stick to short sentences (even for important concepts), and don't be afraid to use dictionaries and other sources to work out how to say your piece, even if it slows you down.[2] There is a lot of pressure in modern Western society to respond to e-mails *now*, but don't let that stop you from taking your time. Your correspondents won't notice a ten-minute difference, even if it feels like an aeon to you.

Once you've decided you're speaking Scandinavian, whatever the context, the first thing to do is to relax. When you do speak, speak slowly. Give yourself time to think if you need it. Use short sentences, and go easy on relative clauses, so you keep your grammar simple. It might not sound completely natural to your listeners, but better a bit stilted than so wrong they struggle to follow. If you're not sure of a word, drop the English term into a Scandinavian sentence. As a fellow Germanic languages with many similar loan words, there is a surprising amount of overlap between Scandinavian and English (Haugen, 1976). Of course, this risks your Scandinavian audience switching their conversation to English. While this can be deeply frustrating, it is never meant disparagingly—they're just trying to make your life easier. You don't have to follow their lead, there is nothing wrong, or rude, about sticking to Scandinavian when a native speaker switches to English. A couple more exchanges are typically all that is needed to signal that you want to speak *their* language and have them switch back. Sometimes a short 'I'd like to speak Scandinavian' might be needed to prompt them. If they can't follow you and prefer English, they'll tell you. Having said that, don't be ashamed of taking an offered out if you need it.

Maximising Your Mileage

Once you've learnt more Scandinavian and have started speaking it at the university, how do you convince others you're doing a good job of it? Having a proven track record in the Scandinavian scholarly milieu will impress the people who

CHAPTER EIGHTEEN

Challenges for International PhD Students Studying in Scandinavia

ANDREI ANDRYIEUSKI

Introduction

Every international PhD student arrives to Scandinavia with his or her own cultural background. This chapter presents the typical challenges that PhD students from Eastern Europe (including the former USSR) face when doing a project in Nordic countries. However, the conclusions drawn and the advice given within this chapter can be easily applied to students from other countries.

I am from Belarus, a country that lies (as we Belarusians believe) in the centre of Europe. I came to Denmark for a PhD project in Physics in 2008. Except for great scientific and educational opportunity, coming to and exploring Scandinavia was an excellent cultural experience. I learned a lot of things about myself that I had never thought about before, like things that were typical back home, but rather strange for Scandinavians.

Eastern Europeans: What Are They Like?

To make a portrait of a typical Eastern European, we need to consider the typical conditions in which the personality of an Eastern European forms. Creating such a portrait can illustrate the cultural differences international students can bring with them, aspects of personality and outlook that find their way into the travellers' baggage.

Countries are often compared according to the six parameters developed by the Dutch social psychologist Geert Hofstede (2001). Power distance (inequality of power distribution in the society; the larger the score the more unequal the distribution), individualism (a degree of the society's members interdependence), masculinity (how important achievements and success are), uncertainty avoidance (the measure of how threatening changes in life are), long term orientation (flexibility in dealing with traditions) and indulgence (how weak the control over desire and emotion is).

Denmark and Russia can be compared as the differences are significant. In contrast to the Danes, Russians generally live in a much more unequal society, pay much attention to personal relationships, are more competitive, are afraid of the future, are pragmatic in relation to traditions and norms, and feel that indulging themselves is wrong (a low level of indulgence correlates with cynicism and pessimism).

Broadly speaking, Eastern Europeans do not trust others, or even themselves. They are afraid of possible punishment because of undesirable points of view or actions, so they prefer to not be socially active. Many are afraid of quick life changes and an unpredictable future, and many are not making long-term plans, since they are perceived as never coming true (Kirienko, 2004).

Eastern Europeans who start their PhD studies are not 'typical' Eastern Europeans. First of all, they are very good students, the ones who are called 'crammers' by their schoolmates. The educational load is much higher in Eastern Europe from the beginning of school studies, and it is huge at universities. Thus, good Eastern European students are usually extremely hard-working, but at the same time a lot of them lack self-confidence and are perfectionists.

These students have to learn to make a thorough analysis of time and effort, to set priorities and to spread the load throughout the semester—skills and practices that are not always developed in Eastern European schooling. This presents a new challenge to many students. There is a special Eastern European time management used called, *mobilization type of activity*. Students can procrastinate until the very deadline and then struggle hard without sleeping three nights in a row trying to finalize the report.

The student from Eastern Europe is free to choose when to learn, but they have little control over what subjects to learn. As soon as they start a certain educational line (specialty), a set of classes to attend is determined. The courses at many Eastern European universities give a very good background on basic 'must-have' subjects, but there is a lack of advanced topics. Many professors teach the same courses for decades without taking into account new discoveries and concepts. A lot of them may not be doing active research, since the teaching load on professors is large. In addition, the natural sciences can suffer from the lack of modern equipment; as a result, the students may have heard about PCR-machines (important instruments for molecular biologists) or cleanrooms (special laboratories for micro and nanofabrication with extremely clean air), but never used them. As a consequence, the education tends to be too theoretical (Aukes, 2006).

Professors at universities are considered as bosses (recall Hofstede's 'high power inequality'), so it is not typical that students dispute with them or evaluate their courses. The supervisors are expected to guide the students, and the students are expected to implement the decisions and ideas of the supervisor.

Marks and ratings are very important: they do not only give prestige and satisfy a hunger for competition, but are the key factors determining whether one gets a scholarship and a room in a dormitory.

Culturally, the typical Eastern European doctoral student is a timid hardworking perfectionist who expects guidance from their supervisor. But no matter which place on Earth a person comes from, they bring certain practices and beliefs when travelling to Scandinavia. These cultural traits can be useful, useless, or even present some challenges for a person in a new cultural surrounding. In the following sections, I focus on the typical challenges that many international PhD students face and offer advice on how to overcome them.

Challenge 1: Interaction with Others

Do You Speak English?

In the time of the Soviet Union, students learned English at schools and universities. There was, however, a special manner of teaching English to students, so that they were able to read, but unable to speak. Indeed, why should one be able to talk to foreigners from the other side of the iron curtain if all of them were spies? There is no longer a Soviet Union, but this method of teaching has been carefully preserved. Thus, the English interview may become a real challenge for a PhD candidate, and it is better to worry about spoken English well in advance from the first years of university studies. Luckily, there are plenty of private courses with modern programs that are very efficient in training oral language.

If a person is accepted for a PhD position, he or she has to learn a new scientific topic with new terminology that is a challenge in itself. Not knowing 'ordinary life' English, it becomes difficult to participate in small talk at coffee or lunch breaks, and may lead to a certain degree of social isolation.

Prepare in advance. Learn English. Watch English movies without translation. Participate in English speaking summer schools, 'work-and-travel' programs, volunteer camps and internships during university years. It will pay off hundredfold.

There are plenty of free and paid educational resources on the internet, such as, https://www.eslpod.com, https://esllibrary.com/, and language courses within the massive open online courses aggregated on https://www.coursera.org/, https://www.edx.org/, https://www.udacity.com/, http://www.mooec.com and https://www.futurelearn.com.

Interaction with the Supervisor

Scandinavia is widely known for a non-hierarchical structure at the working place, and a more egalitarian work culture. Basically, the authority is based on professionalism and the supervisor is regarded not as a boss, but as a coach (Theis, 2013). The first thing that often shocks an international student is the manner to address a person with more seniority by the first name only. In my Eastern European homeland, you call an older or more experienced person using both the first name and father's name, something like 'Ivan Petrovich'. It took a few months for me to get used to this informal first name calling, and in the transition time I even avoided calling my supervisor by any name at all when addressing him.

Many Eastern European students experience difficulties in understanding and expressing their wishes and feelings. Many are afraid of mistakes and prefer not to show that something is going wrong. As a result, they prefer to contact the supervisor as little as possible, hiding themselves in the secure shelters of offices and labs.

Performance evaluation interviews[1] are very uncommon for Eastern Europe, and it takes some time for students to adapt to this kind of interaction (which may be the reason why some universities even suggest short courses on employee appraisal interview). In principle, Eastern European students can communicate their troubles directly, but that may happen when a certain (typically high) threshold of discomfort is reached after a long period of time. Then they may tell everything very emotionally, like an emotional avalanche. The calm Scandinavian ways of negotiation and communication is not very typical for Eastern Europeans. Learn how to do this, as I have found that the Scandinavians I worked with appreciate it very much.

An Eastern European student expects direct orders from a supervisor, but in Scandinavia instead of this he or she hears something like, 'this is the plan and now it is up to you how to follow it'. It can be shocking when you hear a Scandinavian PhD student reply to a Scandinavian supervisor: 'Have you said everything you wanted, professor? Now I will go and make the experiment my own way.' A Scandinavian supervisor may not always give straight directions; he or she is more like a coach, which may bring an international PhD student to frustration. Some students say 'I wish my professor was stricter and more authoritarian, as this is the

pre-service teacher-training courses, and thesis supervision at the undergraduate level. She can be contacted at cce@du.se.

Louise Floor Frellsen (PhD) completed her doctorate from the Technical University of Denmark on the topic of integrated nanophotonics. She used to think that all the paperwork was a pointless bother until she joined the PhD committee. Now she would really like to share what she found out working there so that others might also see how the requirements from the PhD school can really help the student.

Julian Geiger (PhD) has studied biochemistry in Tuebingen, Germany, before he started his PhD in Molecular Biology at Roskilde University in Denmark in 2014. In his recently submitted thesis, he looked at the impact of microRNAs on mitochondrial metabolism in insulin-secreting cells. After defending the thesis in summer 2017, Julian has plans to move back to Germany where he can be contacted at jug01@gmx.de.

Kamma Overgaard Hansen (PhD) has a doctorate in Art History. Her PhD project was facilitated as a partnership between Aarhus University and Horsens Art Museum in Denmark and concerns Danish Art of the 1980s. Kamma has previously been employed as Art Curator at Horsens Art Museum, project leader in a social organization, and communicator at a clinic for Occupational Medicine. She is currently teaching Cultural Communication at Aarhus University.

Anne Vorre Hansen (PhD) has a doctorate in Business Administration/Service Innovation, and is currently a Research Assistant at Roskilde University and a self-employed consultant. Anne Vorre holds a M.Sc. in Anthropology, and has years of experience as a consultant of user-driven innovation processes in the private and public sector and as a researcher and project manager of service innovation. In her current research, she focuses on service innovation and value co-creation—applying a critical view on the empirical and analytical applicability of the concepts.

Roope A. Kallionpää works as a doctoral student in the University of Turku, Finland. His research focuses on the cancer-predisposition syndrome neurofibromatosis type 1 encompassing molecular and cell biology, as well as epidemiology of the disorder. Roope received an MSc (pharm) degree from the University of Helsinki, Finland, in 2014, majoring in pharmaceutical chemistry. During the studies, he worked with organic synthesis and enzymes involved in steroid metabolism.

Andreas Kamstrup studied philosophy and organisation and is now a PhD Fellow at Copenhagen Business School, Department of Organization, where he examines how digital technologies influence work. In cooperation with the Danish Architecture Centre, he has been examining how a digital platform designed to create innovations within the built environment operates. Andreas has a specific interest in how the expanding digitalisation of work processes creates new forms of collaboration and competition. Recently, he has examined this in the technology industries of Silicon Valley through a research stay at Stanford University.

Simon Krogh (PhD) worked for several years as a communication specialist in IBM and various consultant firms prior to returning to academia. He completed a PhD in Organizational Change from Copenhagen Business School in Denmark. The thesis was an in-depth study of the organizational consequences of introducing new technology in the health sector. He is currently coordinating and teaching BA and MA level courses in Communication and Organization at Copenhagen Business School, Denmark. He can be contacted at simon.krogh@live.dk.

Christopher McMaster (PhD) has been lead editor on all editions of the 'Survive and Succeed' series. He completed a PhD in education from the University of Canterbury in Christchurch, New Zealand. His thesis was based on a critical ethnography of developing inclusive culture in an Aotearoa New Zealand high school. He has taught at the primary, secondary, and tertiary levels in the USA, UK and New Zealand. Christopher was most recently an Assistant Professor of Education at Augsburg College, Minneapolis, USA. He now lives in New Zealand, developing a model of alternative education within a mainstream high school, and can be contacted at drchrismcmaster@gmail.com.

Caterina Murphy (PhD) has been the editing partner across the global 'Survive and Succeed' series of books. She has a Master of Education (Hons) from Massey University and a PhD (Indigenous Studies) from Te Whare Wānanga o Awanuiārangi. Mentoring and lifting the aspirations of others is her passion. Her professional and research interests include career counselling, early years' education, teaching practice, mentoring, qualitative research, gifted education and oral history methodology. She is currently the Head of Enhanced Learning at Edgecumbe College. This is her eighth edited book and she can be contacted at academicexpressnz@xtra.co.nz.

Luke John Murphy (PhD) holds a doctorate in the History of Religion from Aarhus University in Denmark, where he worked on the difficulties of delineating pre-Christian religions in Iron Age Scandinavia. Originally from the British Isles, he has taught at institutions in Germany, Iceland, and Denmark, and is taking up a Bernadotte Post-Doctoral Research Fellowship at Stockholm

University, Sweden, from 2017. He can be contacted at luke@luke-murphy.com.

Julie A. Niziurski is an American studying abroad in Denmark. She obtained her Masters degree in psychology from the University of Texas at San Antonio and is currently working on her PhD in psychology at Aarhus University. Her dissertation focuses on the relationship of emotion and memory. She is now enjoying living in Aarhus, Denmark and can be contacted at Julie@psy.au.dk.

BethAnne Paulsrud (PhD) earned her doctorate in Educational Science in Languages and Language Development at Stockholm University, Sweden, with a thesis on English-medium instruction in Swedish upper secondary schools. She is an Assistant Professor of English at Dalarna University, currently working as a Postdoctoral Researcher at the Centre for Research on Bilingualism, Stockholm University. Dr. Paulsrud's teaching includes courses in English and pre-service teacher training. Her research interests include multilingualism and policy in education. She can be reached at byp@du.se.

Carsten Lund Pedersen (PhD) is a Postdoc at the Copenhagen Business School, Denmark, where he researches project-based strategies and employee autonomy. He similarly completed his industrial PhD in strategic responsiveness from the Copenhagen Business School, in collaboration with a major telecommunications company. He has previously been a visiting PhD student at MIT Sloan School of Management. Moreover, he is involved with teaching in executive programmes within Business development. He can be contacted at cp.smg@cbs.dk.

Laurie Prange (Prange-Martin) is a PhD candidate at Aalborg University (AAU) in Denmark in Business Economics and lives in Vancouver, British Columbia with her husband and son. The family recently located to southern Canada after sixteen years in Whitehorse, Yukon and they are enjoying the change in weather. Before becoming a full-time student, she was a tenured college faculty member for fifteen years as a professional librarian, coordinator, and instructor. She holds a Master of Education specializing in Information Technology from Memorial University in Newfoundland (MUN) and a Master of Library and Information Science from University of Western Ontario (UWO).

Bethany Rogers is a food historian and Scandinavian studies enthusiast. She completed an MA in Medieval Icelandic Studies from the University of Iceland, in addition to an MA.Ed. in Secondary Education and a B.S. in News-editorial journalism at other institutions. Her thesis is an exploration of the cultural and anthropological importance of dairy products in medieval Iceland. She has taught a variety of topics from Computer Science to English Literature to students from age five to adult in Taiwan, the United States and Iceland. She lives in Reykjavik, Iceland, and can be contacted at blr3@hi.is.

Jakob Rosenkrantz de Lasson (PhD) is a Danish engineer in physics and nanotechnology, and obtained his PhD in nanophotonics (2015) from the Technical University of Denmark. In 2016, he joined the company TICRA in Copenhagen in a position as research engineer, where he currently focuses on consulting and R&D on antennas for satellites and space missions. Jakob is a co-editor on this Nordic edition in the 'Survive and Succeed' series.

Sharon Stein is a doctoral candidate in the Department of Educational Studies at the University of British Columbia. Her work examines trends in the privatization and internationalization of higher education by linking contemporary developments to transnational colonial histories and ongoing patterns of uneven global engagement. She is committed to pluralising imaginaries of global justice and social change. Her work has been published in Higher Education, Review of Higher Education, and Critical Studies in Education.

Lene Tanggaard (PhD) is Professor of Psychology in the Department of Communication and Psychology, Aalborg University, Denmark, where she serves as Vice Head of Department, advisor for several PhD students, Co-director of The International Centre for the Cultural Psychology of Creativity (ICCPC), and co-director of the Center for Qualitative Studies. She is regional editor of The International Journal of Qualitative Research in Education and co-author to the book *A Survival Kit for Doctoral Students and their Supervisors* with Charlotte Wegener.

Natasha A. Webster (PhD) completed her doctorate in Human Geography at Stockholm University in the Fall of 2016. Originally from Canada, Natasha started her PhD two years after migrating to Sweden. While a PhD candidate, she had two children and two maternity leaves while completing her PhD in the 5-year term. Natasha is currently a post-doctoral researcher in a project examining opportunities and obstacles for women migrant entrepreneurs in Sweden.

Charlotte Wegener (PhD) is associate professor in the Department of Communication and Psychology, Aalborg University, Denmark. She is passionate about writing and seeks to expand academic writing as both process and product by involving fiction, music, dreams, and everyday life experiences. She has co-authored *The Open Book: Stories of Academic Life and Writing or Where We Know Things* and is co-founder of the Open Writing Community—a project devoted to making academic writing more democratic, open, and joyful.

www.ingramcontent.com/pod-product-compliance
Ingram Content Group UK Ltd.
Pitfield, Milton Keynes, MK11 3LW, UK
UKHW021009120926
8556IPUK00029B/441

9 781433 148231